The Testimony of my life

Jesus Princess

THE TESTIMONY OF MY LIFE

iUniverse books may be ordered through booksellers or by contacting:

iUniverse
1663 Liberty Drive
Bloomington, IN 47403
www.iuniverse.com
844-349-9409

Because of the dynamic nature of the Internet, any web addresses or links contained in this book may have changed since publication and may no longer be valid. The views expressed in this work are solely those of the author and do not necessarily reflect the views of the publisher, and the publisher hereby disclaims any responsibility for them.

Any people depicted in stock imagery provided by Getty Images are models, and such images are being used for illustrative purposes only. Certain stock imagery © Getty Images.

ISBN: 978-1-6632-5181-7 (sc)
ISBN: 978-1-6632-5180-0 (e)

Library of Congress Control Number: 2023905139

Print information available on the last page.

iUniverse rev. date: 03/31/2023

Introduction

I share my personal life story with you in order for young people to not make the same mistake that I made when I was younger. It's about the first so-called relationship that I had. The young man that I dated was a player in disguise like an angel, but I felt for his game. He was so good at what he was doing unfortunately felt for his game. I got played by him because I was blindly in love with his charm. I didn't have anybody to talk about what doing. I lived with my aunt at the time, didn't have communication with her. The young man was my aunt friend, but when we had the so-called relationship, he didn't want for our parents to know about it. I didn't know how relationship goes. Maybe if I spoke to someone about it, it would've been differently. My heart would not been broken in the first place. I was lacked knowledge of how to be in a relationship, and the Words of God.

Like Hosea 4:6 says: My people are destroyed from lack of knowledge". "Like Hosea 4:6 says: My people are destroyed from lack of knowledge". The lack of knowledge of the Words of God would get you to a lot of trouble. As Jesus's princess, I should've known better what my fathers' Words says in Joshua 1:8. This book of the law shall not depart out of thy mouth— The law which had already been written by Moses, and from which he and the people were to take all those precepts by which their lives were to be governed. Though there was a copy of the law laid up in the sanctuary, yet this was not sufficient. We need to have a friend that we could trust and talk to. Do not be secretive when it comes to relationship. The princess got herself into trouble because she didn't talk to anybody while she was in that mess. She failed to talk to her Heavenly father at the time. All she did was to believe in something that she had no idea of it is. John 10: The thief does not come except to steal, and to kill, and to destroy. I have come that they may have life, and that they may have it more abundantly. In this World that we're living in trust in no one, but Jesus. Jesus will never forsake us nor leaving us. Jesus is enough for anyone who need a friend. The princess didn't know about relationship, but she could've talked to someone who is more experience than her, but she paid the consequences dearly. Talking to somebody doesn't mean that person is your friend. Don't be secretive in life. Whatever need to know, God is waiting for you to talk to Him, and He will show you what need to know. God speaks in different ways. Trust Jesus-Christ in everything like Job 33:14-15 says; "https://www. kingjamesbibleonline.org/Job-33-14/"14For God speaketh once, yea twice, yet man perceived it not. "https://www.kingjamesbibleonline. org/Job-33-15/"15In a dream, in a vision of the night, when deep sleep falleth upon men, in slumberings upon the bed; The one that we think is our friends may not be a real friend."

God will reveal everything we need to know in this life to us, therefore do not hope on anybody else, but God. The only person who loves you is Jesus. John 3:16 For God so loved the world that he gave his one and only Son, that whoever believes in him shall not perish but have eternal life. The love that we need is the love of God, then will know what love truly is.

He called us friends when the enemy is treating his servant horses, things name it. He never presents when something bad happen to his worshipers. The word that he uses for them is "if he was there his horse would never die. Jesus always with you every day till the end of this world. He promised us that in Matthew 28:19-20 "Therefore go and make disciples of all nations, baptizing them in the name of the Father and the Son and the Holy Spirit,20 and teaching them to obey everything I have commanded you. Listen to this "And surely I am with you always, to the very end of the age." "Jesus will never leave you nor forsake you. He shows it to me in my experience even though I didn't know what His Words say. I had the accident when I was seeking for God after my heart was crushed by a so call my best friend.

He also shows it to me what the Psalmist said in Psalms 91:9-12 If you say, The Lord is my refuge, and make the Most High your dwelling,10 no harm will overtake you, no disaster will come near your tent.11 For He will command His angels concerning you to guard you in all your ways; they will lift you up in their hands, so you will not strike your foot against a stone. Isn't God great. Psalmist David also says in Psalms 34:7 The angels of the Lord encamp around those who fear him, and he delivers them. If what it says in that verse wasn't true, I would be here today; I would've been in the grave by now. Let me go back to my track of the book.

It's up to the man who's going to propose to me. I'm not going to propose to myself it's not because I didn't have an answer for him, but I thought it was a silly question. The answer that I had for him was around 25 or 26 years old, but I told him I didn't know. I asked him a question myself "do you think I will be a good wife someday, and he answered of course you will be a wonderful wife.

I know that he didn't really love me as he said. So ever since then I could never trust or date anybody ever again It was so hard on me. Everyone that I share this story with was asking me to move one with my life. I even said that "I would never date anyone ever again." I was so scared, and thought that every man where the same. I even said to myself since my first experience went down the drill just like that when I need a kid all I'm going to is to buy a sperm at the hospital, and pay the doctor to inject it inside of me just to have a baby.

When I thought about it; I said forget it because it's not going to be fair for a baby to be raised with only one parent. I thought like that because I didn't want to get hurt again; that wasn't a way for me to think. As a Christian my God can bring true happiness in my life. I should've trust God more instead of thinking of this stupid idea. The reason why things like that happened to me was because before I put myself in the situation, I didn't consult God for His guidance. Now I'm so scared that anybody that I think that everyone is the same, but I realized that I have to let God take over my life completely. My heart is too small for it to be broken again. I can't take another heartbroken anymore

It was so hurt that I seek for God's mercy. I seek the Lord for help which was a very good thing that I did. I've been so humiliated by him because of his girlfriend. They are married now, so I believe that he wasn't the one for me. I believe that God will send me the right prince in my life, and I'm waiting for him. Someone who never going to lie to me no matter how bad the situation may seem to be. Before I said to myself that I didn't need a man to come to my life anymore because I got myself. God knew what I was thinking about, and sent a pastor to House of Prayers to preach for some reason he started preaching about masturbation "how it is a sin." I felt like God was talking to me because when I said I didn't need any man in my life because I thought of doing that. After the service I went to the pastor to explain my situation, and how God used him to deliver me this message. After listening to my story, he thinks God and prayed with me ever since then I give myself completely to Christ, and got baptized. What I'm trying to say is that there are some situations that you're going through God is waiting for you to surrendered your life to Him. God want to save you from something that you're deep in which is so against God's laws. He let something it happened to you to get your full attentions. You might say that you're never going to trust a man in your life ever, but learn to trust God and He will send the right person in your life in His time. God is the boss of my life right now and forever, so please don't think like I thought before I surrendered my life to Christ Jesus. Let God take control over your life.2 Peter 3:8-9 "8 But, beloved, do not forget this one thing, that with the Lord one day a as a thousand years, and a thousand years as one day. 9 The Lord is not slack concerning His promise, as some count slackness, but is longsuffering toward us, not willing that any should perish but that all should come to repentance. Let God do His perfect work in your life, and you will not be disappointed.

I hate lies so much that anybody could pull a gun trigger in my head, but do not to lie to me. Because lying to me could kill me and anyone that lie is the devil child says "John 8:44 You belong to your father, the devil, and you want to carry out your father's desires. He was a murderer from the beginning, not holding to the truth, for there is no truth in him. When he lies, he speaks his native language, for he is a liar and the father of lies". Now on my thirties, my family is pressuring me to look for a man to marry me. I told them that I don't believe in taking chances with love. For them, all they saw was to get married just to have a child without looking at the consequences of being in a relationship without the Will of God in my life. The reason why what they were saying didn't move me was because I believe that God has a plan for me, and if I didn't die when the car structed me, I have to be patient to wait on God. When I spoke to them like that, they mocked me by saying will God come down on earth to hand me a man? They also said that at my age scientist says that I won't be able to bare children. I rebuke every negative word they have spoken unto my life in the Name of Jesus. They called me Ms. Jesus. Don't let anyone pressure you onto doing anything just because of what are they thinking. Because of that man I've been persecuting by his wife every time she got a chance to, but I am not afraid of the persecutions. The words of God clearly say in "2 Timothy 3:12 ¹² Yea, and all that will live godly in Christ Jesus shall suffer persecution." I am not afraid of the persecutions. I remembered a Sunday after church before the accident the wife told me that, Did I know that God loves me? After saying that, she said to me whatever I'm serving just keep it up. I didn't understand what was she talking about until now the Holy Spirit stopped a service just for me to tell Satan's agent "Isaiah 7:7 Thus saith the Lord GOD, it shall not stand, neither shall it come to pass. Isaiahb54: ¹⁷ No weapon that is formed against thee shall prosper; and every tongue that shall rise against thee in judgment thou shalt condemn. This is the heritage of the servants of the LORD, and their righteousness is of me, saith the LORD."

The Testimony of My Life

I grew up in Haiti, at 15 years of age there was a boy my age that always came to play basketball in my yard. He always tried to get to me, but I was not so easy to get to. The boy was dating 4 of my girlfriends at the same time. When I knew that I was always mean to him because I didn't want him to think that he had a chance with me.

He created chaos between those girls who were raised together. When he tried to approach me, I always gave him the character that I always used toward him, and fled like the devil before me. If you read the book of James 4:7 says "Submit yourselves therefore to God. Resist the devil, and he will flee from you."

I always love God, but at the time I wasn't a born-again Christian yet. But he was always trying to come close to me, but I never gave him a chance to. So, he came to the United States in 2003. I never heard from him since then "thank God. "Talking about being a born again Christian when I always went to revival, and they called whoever want to give Christ their life, I was always the first one to go to accept Jesus.

Yet I didn't know what does it mean to be a born again until I came to the United States in 2004. I used to live in Orlando Florida for three years. My dad was a member of the First Methodist church in Orlando leading by Pastor Joseph Anthony the brother of Joseph Jacques Taylor. As they had a group going from house to house to pray, I decided again to give my life to Christ even though I didn't what that meant, and loved

1

to surround my life to Christ. I didn't get to baptize over there because my family moved to Georgia, and I moved to NJ.

Moving to NJ was the best thing in my life because it was where my church pastor was preaching, and mentioned what being born again meant. After that sermon I gave my name to get baptized. There was a very nice young man in my church that saw me, and he didn't know how to talk to me because I had the mean character in my face always. We were in the youth choir together, but he was not my friend. I didn't talk to everybody, and never called them my friend just because we had a conversation once or twice. I didn't trust people like that to call them my friend. A lot of people thought I was conceited. Maybe if I wasn't as such, I would've had someone who has experience on relationship to tell me how does relationship works.

He got to talk to me because one of my fellow brethren in church was getting married, and invited me to be a bridesmaid at his wedding. I agreed to be the bride's maid, and it turned out that the young man was the instructor to teach us what to do, and how to walk at the wedding. The groom gave him my phone number, and also gave me his phone number as well. Ever since then we became good friend in fact, he was my best friend. We used to talk about everything and anything. I was so close with him that my girlfriend used me to talk to him for her because she had a crush on him. Based on that talked every time because I was their messenger. I didn't know that he/I would've felt for each other. My goal was to be a married and family therapy. Therefore, being in the middle of them made me use my skill, but the feedback I got from him for my girlfriend/ cousin was not pleasant. Whenever she gave a message for him, I told him exactly what she said, but his answer was never good. As a counselor, I could never tell her what was his answer. We spoke so much on the phone, I enjoyed it yet we were not in a relationship. He started telling his feelings for me, and I didn't show him that I liked him because I was playing a role of messenger. Day and night we were on the phone un-separable. When he was at work, we were always on the phone. When he got out of work at midnight, he always needed to see me even beg to see me. Well, I let him to come see me, and when he came, we talk held hands, and he went home. That was all I needed just to have conversation with him that was never end.

I could say that we had a relationship not even married couples in this day have. We started dating each order; go to places together all the time such as "movie, and other places, and I thought that for the first time in my life I had a boyfriend. The young man knows exactly what he was doing. I used to watch HBO a lot there was a show called Real Sex on HBO. They used to show how to kiss for the first time in it, and I learned what to do from that show. There was a prayer that I did, and forget about it. I didn't pray out loud for anyone to hear me, but I asked God accomplished with him.

I was only 23 years old when I had my first kiss at the time. And prayed God that whoever I let to kiss me first that would be a sign he is the one. For some reason he was the only man that I let kissed me. The biggest mistake that I made is to invite Jesus so late into that mess. Even I was surprised as he was because he knows that I would've pushed him, and surprisingly I didn't push him. I didn't know what it was the only thing that I thought off that he was the one, and The Holy Spirit reminded me of the prayer I made. When the thing was going that way, I mean it was also a mistake not to tell our parents about it as well just because he was asking me for a little more time.

I didn't know what it meant at the time until it was too late after I went so far in a thing that I didn't know what it was. That's why people who knew about asked him He still have an argument to tell them "No he didn't have any relationship with me." Only God knows what was going on. He makes me feel like a dirty liar for years now. I regretted that I let all that happened, and so hurt because he could've told me the truth about what he was doing. The truth never hurt me it is the lies that's killed me. God healed my broken hearted; thank you Lord. Let me tell you what he said to me after our first kiss.

The first time we kissed; he called me to tell me that I lied to him because I told him that I didn't know how to kiss, and never kissed before. But I was a good kisser. I was so surprised to hear that, but I didn't know how to explain to him how did I learned to kiss because at I was so embarrassed to tell him that I learned it from a TV show. Ever since then school's out. We started doing things that I didn't even know that I could do, and he was always told me that he loved me.

The first time he used the "Love word to me in the phone I was so shocked to hear him said it to me, and I asked have you been drinking? He answered why did you ask that, and I said to him "you told me that you loved me, and he said I meant it too as we were finished talking in the phone, I texted him that I loved him as well.

He was so convincing at that time because I used to love acting. I remembered one time I asked him: ok you said that you loved me, but I love acting so what if my career send to L.A California what are you going to do? And he told me that is not a problem I'm willing to move to L.A with you, so I asked him "what about his parents? and he said to me that they will be fine.

And I asked him a second question of some scene asked you to kiss your partner, so "what are you going to do about that? he answered me that it just a scene which is not a problem because I know that my wife would be with me after the scene. I was so convinced by his answered that he must really love me, so I felt for all this trick, and I loved him even more. In July,2010 I went to L.A on vacation, and he was the one who drove me to the place where I was supposed to meet my friends that I was going with.

The reason why I felt for his trick was because a girlfriend of mine had a big crush on him, so she told me about it because at the time we weren't in a relationship yet. I told him about the crush that my girlfriend had on him, so he told me that he didn't feel that it was me that he loved.

I didn't believe him that's when he became with the idea, I didn't like him. I agreed that he said I didn't like him because I was secretly in love with him. To prove something to him right before my friend I gave him a hickey; he still didn't get it. The thing is I never tried that on anybody before but him since then I tried to show him my feelings for him, but he still didn't get it.

Remember that he told me to behave in L. A when I went to L. A, he ends up making out with my girlfriend and she was so happy about it she called me in L. A to tell me about it. When I came back from L. A I asked him, and he denied it. He just tells me that my girlfriend needed a ride, so he gave her the ride after dropping her she just gave him a kiss.

My girlfriend told me about the kiss; it wasn't just any kiss. it was a French kiss that got them to made out. Back then we were not in a relationship, so I was happy for her because she told me that she likes him. When my girlfriend told me about it, I didn't tell her anything about how I felt about him, and how much I missed him because I was six hours away from him. Since that happened between them, I didn't think that he really like me yeah, I say liked and not loved. After showing me that he was not interested in my friend; I decided to show him how I really felt about him, and yet he still didn't get it. Long story short.

One Sunday the ex-girlfriend at the time, who is now his wife came to the church just to spy on me. When I saw her what I asked him was that "you could've told me that you were having a visitor since we were dating."

And he told me that even he didn't know that she was coming to visit the church. In the next month he told me that he was back with her; in that month she started coming to the church. She made up that big lie about me; then I used to go the restroom a lot, and she followed me to the restroom. As I was using the lady's room, and she came inside the restroom fixing her cloths for minutes.

When I came out of the room that I was in; I saw her still there, and I said to her you look so beautiful who told that your cloths were not fixed because I saw come in a long time. And she told me that it's the legend that she was fixing, and she went out crying telling people that I said she was a mess. God knows that was a lied, and for a second time I went to the restroom again two people was following me; they told me that they didn't like the fact I made their friend cried.

They didn't believe me even him didn't believe me either because I used to act so tough with him because of the lies that he used to tell me, so it was her words against mine. Yeah, I had a big mouth just to make him thought that I was a troublemaker that's why he didn't believe me. After that he didn't talk to me for a long time because she told him that

I made her cry. I used to love acting, but she was a good actress than me with her fake cried.

God knew that I didn't do that to her, and I would've never fight over a man because it's not worth it, and I am not the kind of desperate girl to do that. It's one thing that I will never do is fighting over man. Why go through all this trouble over a man that love you, and you love. If he is yours you don't have to create all this trouble just to make another person look bad. And I could say that he was hers because they now married, and having the life that God wanted them to have.

He was a good guy, but I would never go to all this for him, that's why he didn't think that I loved him because I told him about the big crushed that my girlfriend had for him, and I seemed to be a trouble maker. I believe that was why he told me that I was the one who sent him where he was. He knows that wasn't true because he took, and made the decision that he wanted; choosing the woman that he loved.

He didn't have to make all these excuses all he had to do was to tell me truth, and I would've been fine instead he gave me all the excuses that is written in the book of excuses. Ouch! that was hurt through my bones anyway forget it; it's the past and what happened in the past stay in the past. "I don't want to wake up the sleeping cat, so moved on with his life so should I.

To continue with the act that she came off with. Honestly, I didn't know what they were talking about, so I went to the bathroom hitting my head on the walls, asking God what was happening? The Holy Spirit told me "Do not worry it just an act. After church I went home still crying and praying God. God told me that everything was going to be alright.

I remembered that he told me to behave, and when I got there all my friends was going to party, and met famous people just because he told me to behave, I always stayed in the hotel room reading my bible before I slept. My step sister told me "Why did you come to a vacation in L.A, and you don't want to enjoy it? "She said to me that she would never bring me to vacation ever again.

The thing was that I couldn't have fun without my best friend. I didn't have fun over there because I missed my best friend. We used to talk every second, and my phone was disconnected then I couldn't speak to him at all that was then I realized how much I loved him, and missed him. At this time if he told me not to go, I wouldn't go no matter how famous I wanted to be as an actress.

It was the first time I felt so connected to somebody in my life. Not even my mother, and father that left me for so long. I wasn't raised by my mother, or father, but I didn't miss them like that. He made me feel that way; a way I never understand why for the first time in my life. And speaking of behave I tried to behave, but he wasn't behaving behind my back because he was being a hypocrite at the time. I'm not going into details about his behavior; just think about it even when I asked him about his behavior behind me; he was always denied what happened. My heart was bleeding, but I couldn't tell him about it because he was in denial.

I tried to ask him about it because the night it happened my friend called me in my step sister phone. My friend didn't know that loved him because never told her about it when she told me about what happened, and talk to him about it he was till denial it. Ever since then I couldn't trust him anymore no matter how much I loved him. I loved him so much I tried everything with him just for him not to stray, but he was a stray puppy.

But only one thing because of what the bible said about that particular thing I am not supposed to do before marriage, so I wasn't going to do it with him, so he didn't think that I loved him after I agreed to do all those stupid things. Now I learned something really powerful in Sunday school when we were studying; Learned to love; and I now understand the meaning of love. After the teacher did a lot of research about the lesson, he came with a lot of definitions about love which made me felt that I was being played by my ex-best friend.

Love is action not that inching that you have in your flesh. Read 1 Corinthians 13;1-4 you will see what is the true meaning of Love. In John 3;16 says that For God so loved the world, that He gave His only Son, that whoever believes in Him should not perish but have Eternal life.

This is the kind of action that I mentioned about the love is action. God made an action to show us His love for us. Think about it carefully girls because they are deceivers out there. When you meet someone that you think you love, so please go to God and prayers to ask Him for direction. He is faithful to give you the direction that you ask him for. I remembered after my accident I was in a rehab, and one of my friends brought a phone for me, and my ex-friend was the first person that I called with it.

Because all I knew that I was in a rehab, but I didn't understand what was happening to me. As I called him, he didn't answer his phone for some reason, and I called him a second time. Since we were best friends before we used to talk about anything, so I thought that we were still friends. When he answered his phone; he was the one who explained everything to me because I had no clue of what happened.

I thought everything was ok between us, and I received a text from him that he was sending to his girlfriend, so the text went like this; boo she called me twice this morning, the text went straight to my phone messages, and I texted him back said that it was ok. When I texted him back, he told me that he was sorry because he was sending the text to his girlfriend, so I told him that I figured it.

I'm sorry for texting him, or called him because I didn't know he had a report to give to her. That's when the friend that invited me to walk at his wedding told me that "you cannot love him because he's engaged if you still love him, it is like you love a married man. I was so surprised about that, and felt betrayed all over.

Before he got married even my own family was spying on me for him because I told them that I was still loved him for some reason. That person thought that I didn't know what she was doing, but she was wrong because she told my spiritual mother about me said that "For some reason I felt deeply loved him."

After a while before his wedding, she was driving me to her house asked me this silly question; do you still love him, so I asked myself why did she ask me this question? Even though I loved him; I crossed my fingers told to her "No because the man is getting married why should I tell her that I loved him still. "Love don't just go away like that, and she and his fiancé are the best of friends why did she ask me that question.

Even after all that I was so hurt, and explained to my friends, and his family what happened he made them believe that I was crazy because it wasn't true what I told them. Imaging I didn't even had a brain injury then I remember all that after my brain injury; do I look or seem crazy to you people? when they don't love you all that can happen. They could say that you are crazy out of your mind by thinking that they had a relationship with you even if you end up sleeping with them they could say the same thing about you just like my ex-friend makes everybody believe that I was out of my mind.

He didn't even care about me if I loved him or not. Imagine your own family; somebody who said that she cared about me looking for words out of my mouth to brought to them. That's why I pray God to do not let anybody like that come toward me again because I went through too much. I don't want to have any uglier experience with anybody ever again. Somebody who act like he cares about me, and hurt me like that. Seriously I thought that he cared about me, but he was just lying to me from the beginning.

You know what he told me once; you the one who sent me back to her. I didn't understand why did he said so but God alone knows what he meant by that. Now the person that he told me that I sent him to are now his wife, and they are a happy married couple. Honestly, I'm so happy for them. After that experience I don't trust any men ever again, nor date anyone again because there are some actors out there that are ready to deceive many women out there like me who don't have any ideas of what a relationship should be, so be careful on who you trust.

I thought that he cared about me, but I was wrong. That's why I told you guys who read my book "God is the only man that's never leave you, nor forsake you. Let go to Deuteronomy 31:6 to see what It says. Be strong and courageous. Do not be afraid or terrified because of them, for the Lord your God goes with; He will never leave you nor forsake you. Speaking of that verse I remembered one time I was going through this broken hearted, and I went to the Tuesday prayer in my church as I entered the sanctuary the former pastor; God rest his soul;

stop the service, and took the microphone from the leader of the service. He said "my daughter God told me to tell you that He is with you in what you are going through.

I was so surprised, and started crying because I didn't even tell my pastor anything about what I was going through. And I didn't know that God even know me surprisingly I was wrong God knows me even better than I know myself. That made me understand what God told Jeremiah the prophet. In Jeremiah 1:5 Before I formed you in the womb I knew you, before you were born, I set you apart; I appointed you as a prophet to the nations. Praise God.

I remembered in a Sunday school we were studying "What Pouch me to Act the way I did? and one of the points was "Friendship is good as read the lesson I agreed with what the lesson said. I told the class one thing 'I talk to everybody, but everybody could not be my friend, and I told them that the only best friend that I have was Jesus, and He is my only friend as well.' I know what I've been through with earthly people so called my friend, and what the person did to me.

The teacher and some of the students was not agreed with me. They were against my point, so they started to tell me that it is not possible that I don't have any friend. I was well said; the only friend that I have is Jesus because when was going through worst, and crying in my room Jesus is the only One who knows what made the tears in my eyes, and He was the only One I went to. To talk to about my problems sometimes I have tears in my eyes I don't even knows why, but Jesus always know. That's why He was the only friend that I could trust, and He always comfort me and wipes my tears away.

If you need a best friend who understand your pain make Jesus that friend. When you talk to Jesus about your problems; He never calls another person to tell your business. I remembered sent a novel to my pastor that was like this" I have a question for you. Is it a sin to ask God to give me a shut off my flesh desires?

Lately I've been praying God to take that feeling, or my flesh desires away from me because I'm not married, and need to be free from it too. I even thought of never date anyone else ever again because was deceived by somebody that I trusted more than anything in this world.

The reason why I thought like that was because I didn't know Jesus like I do now.

I even thought of when I need a baby, I will just go to a hospital bank where men donate their sperm, and buy one just to have a baby. Then I thought that it is not going to be fair for a child to do not have the love of a father in his or her life. And I said to myself "wait a minute my life is not my own I belong to the Most High God may His Will be done to my life, "and I rebuke that thought from my head. God has a perfect plan for my life, and I know that His perfect plan will be done in my life. Married people get separated, and get a divorce what am I thinking about? God didn't let me died for a reason, so what is the meaning of this?

I never had in my mind to have experiences with men like I'm changing my panties, but I believe that God has a perfect man for me not two or three just one. Beside the one that I used to date did not recognize me as his girlfriend, so that's mean I never had a boyfriend with God patient I will wait for the one who will be my boyfriend and someday my husband until death do us part for real. God is in control of my life may His Will be done.

The man that I trusted, and called my best friend did this to me. What about those men out there that I don't even know? Before I used to think that all men are the same, but that's not true. I was doing my flesh a favor that was not in God Will for me then I messed up, and now I'm waiting for God to say the final word in my life. The man that did this to me is happily married my time is not yet to come, so all I have to do is to be happy for him, and his wife that God had for him.

I'm happy for them honestly, I'm waiting for God to send me my significant one. And I thank God who strengthen me in that experience which I will never let anyone take advantage on me again because my eyes are opened now. The thing is that people who suspected our relationship asked him "what was going on between the two of us, so he lied to them by denied our relationship."

When they asked me, I explained to them what's really happened, and they told me that it's only one thing that could stop him from lying about it; when I asked them what is that? They told me that only if I slept with him and got pregnant by him, and I told them that I never had in my mind to bring kids to this earth in sins because I knew what the Words of God says about that kind of behavior.

It's bad enough that I did all these bad things that could've bring me to have sex with him, and purposely I would've got pregnant by him; imagine how that would've been hurt, and a big shame for me no water could've wash me clean by living a sinful life like that. Thank God I wasn't that stupid even though I did stupid things with him.

As for you men, do not promise a lady something that you can't keep just because you feel like if you promise her those things, she might give you a chance. We as women we have feelings; blood is running through our vein just like you. We do not like being lied to because it's hurt so bad you can't even imagine. I myself went through all of it that's why I'm sharing this with you.

Even the man that told you a million times how much he loves you can give you a lot of excuses why he couldn't be with you when he found his high school sweetheart. I was humiliated so bad by him that I didn't think I wanted to stay in my church anymore because after my accident that was when I even got more humiliated. And God told me clearly "No" I put you in this church not him, so you are not leaving the church because of humiliations.

Remember my Only Son went through worse than you. Read Isaiah 53 verse 3-5 to see what it says. It goes like that:3 He was despised and rejected by men; a man of sorrows, and acquainted with grief; and as one from whom men hide their faces He was despised, and we esteemed Him not.4 Surely, He has borne our griefs and carried our sorrows; yet we esteemed Him stricken, smitten by God, and afflicted.

5 But He was wounded for our transgressions; He was crushed for our iniquities; upon Him was the chastisement that brought us peace, and by His stripes we are healed. I said by His stripes I am healed that's why when people are treating me like a sick person, or a disabled I never like it. They do that just because of my accident the verse 5 of this chapter always give me the strength to tell them to stop treating me like that, because I'm not a broken pieces please don't treat me like that.

As I meditated those verses to my life, I said to myself "why was I troubled myself over this?" Thank God I lived today after being dead in an accident, so I should praise God every second in my life because the life that I'm living is not my own it is Jesus's life that I'm living. Even people that are being married for years got a divorce, or separated "don't feel like life is over for you something would come alone in God time. "I got my strength back as I thought like that. If anyone feel like I felt a while ago just read this passage to see what you're going through is not the End of the World.

God has a better plan for your life just have patient, and you will see what God has in store for your life. I want everyone to know that God is the best lover that I ever have, because He said that He will never leave you nor forsake you, and He didn't live me instead He said to me "In the mess that you are in I'm with you, and He proved that He was with me.

In my accident there He was always by my side hold my hand, talked to me when I needed someone to talk to. I love God with all my heart, my mind, and my soul. Mankind can leave you for another, but God will never leave you. I hope you understand what I'm trying to explain to you, my brethren. He is the only one that love us. The unconditional love come from God alone.

Believe me I know what I'm talking about because I've been there. Even I chose a mankind over Him: He still love me no matter what. No man could ever love you like God does not even your parents. God love you all. The man then that I so call my first love was my best friend because he gave me nothing to worry about since we were always with me. He used to work for a security agency even physically we were not together, but we were always on the phone. After he got off from work at midnight, he always came to see me before he went home.

We fooled around a little bit before he went home, and by the time that he arrived to his house I already miss him. When he got home he always called me to tell me thank you for letting him come over, and how much he already missed me. Before we hang up; we say to each other that we loved each other "he even told me that he loved me in French since he did not speak French, but he did his best to tell me "Je

13

t'aime ma Cherie" which mean I love you my sweetheart, and I said the same thing to him in French as well and we hang up.

I always had the best night when he came around just to talk even though we used to talk every second. Like I said in the introduction. Just because it was like that didn't mean that he was faithful to me. In Psalms 118:8 says It is better to take refuge in the Lord than to trust in humans. Don't ever feel comfortable with anyone like that without the parents know about your relationship with somebody.

Beside don't be like me when your feet mess up in the fowler and think that you can say anything to anybody because they didn't know about it; what was going on between you and the other person. When your heart is broken; it's only you and God that's know what was going on, so keep it between you in God. The person that broke your heart will never tell the truth about what really happened believe me I know what I'm talking about. I know what I'm talking about because I've been through it. That man made everyone think that I was crazy nobody wants that. Just trust in God.

One time I saw that we went too far and need to tell our parents about it, and he told me gave him a little more time. I didn't know what that mean, but always asked him to tell our parents. I didn't know what was in his mind by telling me that to give him a little more time. All this happened not even one of our parents knew about it.

Because I didn't have any experiences in the dating area. I still thought that we were together as a boyfriend, girlfriend. One day I woke up from a dream in that dream I saw his ex-girlfriend be telling people that they were back together as I woke up from the dream, I called him to ask him what was going on between him, and the girl? Because I felt the competition that he put me in, and God showed it to me in a dream; that's was the reason I asked him what was his relationship with the girl.

He asked me "why did you ask?" And I explained the dream to him and he told me "Do not worry because it was just a dream, and I believed him." It was the second weeks of December 2010, and He invited me at a Christmas dinner at his house and his mom invited me to the dinner as well.

We went to the gym together everything was fine. In my 24th birthday he had the plan to bring me, and my friends that I used to work with in a bar. At this time, I told him that bars weren't made for me; I didn't want to go to a bar in that was final. When it was December 25, so his mom didn't see me at the Christmas dinner, and his mom asked him for me; he told his mom a lie that he called me, and I didn't pick up my phone which was a lied.

When his mom asked me why she didn't see me at the dinner? I explained everything to his mother, and I told his mom that I thought that he was a very nice person, and I truly loved him. Reason he never put pressured me to doing anything that I didn't want to do no matter times we were fooling around. Now I understand "why" because he was getting what I told him that I wouldn't do before marriage elsewhere.

And I end up with a broken hearted. What's hurt me most was; he used to tell me that he was confused, but I didn't know why he said so. Until now I see where the confusion came from. While he was dating me, and was also dating his ex-girlfriend which happen to be his wife now. All he had to do was to tell me the truth, and I would've leave him alone. The girl was a wealthy College graduate, and I was a poor girl with no parents that had no job.

Who couldn't even do an essay, so he didn't have to be so confused all he had to tell me that I wasn't his type with no family? I would've understood him. He was not a bad guy, but he decided to hurt the poor girl without a family, and no College degree, nor money. Wow that was really hurt. The thing was he didn't care if he hurts me or not because I didn't worth anything.

I still didn't think of him as a bad person please don't get me wrong about that because things like that happened to poor girl like me considered to be so lazy, and the other girl was a smart graduated with a major in her hand. He helped me taking my Security license officer, but he didn't care of helping me found a job even though he was working as a Security officer.

Because I was nothing to him; I passed the Security test with a score of 98. I applied for job on my security license, but they never called me. It's all good because God is my provider, so I seek for God after being

15

hurt over and over again. God always fix the broken hearted, so He could fix my heart. It's just a long story to keep it short before I lost my track let me go back to where I was after my birthday.

After 18 days would've been his birthday, and by the time I lost my job didn't know what to give him. I was willing to myself to him for the first in my life sleeping with somebody; thank God that didn't happen because if it did happen the accident didn't kill me, but this would've killed me. The reason why I said that would've killed me was because after saving myself for that long, and I had a competition that I felt like I didn't want to lose him.

All this sleeping with him came from the pressured that I had from a girl co-worker that I used to work with, and she always telling all the story about sex that she had every weekend. And on Mondays when we met, she always told me about how good the sex that she had over the weekend was. Since I heard her telling those stories about sex, I felt like I was missing a lot.

Thank God he didn't know that I was planning to give myself to him even though we used to talk about anything and everything, but I kept this from him because I wanted to be a surprise. If that had happened, I would've been dead by now after all these humiliations that I got from him; talking about humiliations he humiliated me for real, truthfully because even after my accident he never talked to me when I could finally go to church for the first time.

Everyone in the church was greeting me asking me; how I was doing, and how did I feel? So, I just saw his back running at the church door. I was so frustrated to see what happened. I called his mom to ask her "what did he say that I done to him"? His mom asked him, and he told his mom that he didn't have anything against me it's the relation with his fiancé that he was protected.

When his mom told me what he said; I prayed God whenever I enter the sanctuary to please make my focus on God alone because my head is not a fan, so I don't want to turn my head in order for my eyes not to meet with his eyes. Ever since I made that prayer when I go to the church even I always the first person to arrive to the church, so I close my eyes until the services end.

That was after my accident; not when I thought of giving myself to him. When I felt like of giving myself to him was before all this accident thing happened. Imagine if I did that stupid thing before my accident how I was so going to regret doing it, and the regretful was going to kill me. Don't be stupid like I was to even think of giving your virginity to anybody before marriage girls. I'm talking to every girl that are reading my book.

The thing is that I never was a disrespected kid that cover all my ugly behavior, but I was living a dirty life that no one knows about. Only God and my ex-best friend knew about because I never kept secret from him at all; because I loved him so much I didn't to keep it from him. But God knows everything even before you talk about what you're thinking about He already know.

Psalmist David says in Psalms 139:1-10 I will give you the verse 1-7; 1 You have searched me, Lord, and you know me. 2 You know when I seat and when I rise; you perceive my thoughts from afar. And the seventh verse says that "Where can I go from your Spirit? Where can I flee from your presence?

The reason why I put that verse is because some of us think that we are smarter than God; I just want to prove you wrong with a capital "Because you can't hide from God. You can do something where the pastor or your family are not going to see you, but God sees and know everything. You can lie to everybody, but you can't lie to God. My parents didn't know about that dirty life I was living, but God knew.

Thank God that stop it before it happened because God knows what was going to happen in the future. My ex-best friend even told me that he wanted to have a child with me, but I told him; no problem to have kids with me, but thing has to be legal because I didn't want to have kids in sins. Even then I thought that he was lying to me, I told him that I loved him as well, but don't lie to me about loving me. He didn't believe that I loved him anyway I fail for his lies. Although he lied to me, I loved him so much I trusted him, and it was a big mistake for trusting him. The lies that he used to tell me for some reason I arrived to a point where I couldn't trust him anymore, and I was right he was doing something in secret.

I thought the reason why he told me that he wanted to have a baby with me was because he wanted to get me pregnant for him to get out of the mess that he put himself into. If he got me pregnant so he was going to force to marry me which was the last thing that I want. I loved him for him not for what he got. All he had to do was to be honest with me. If he was honest with me, I could've deal with the situation, but he chose to lie to me instead. I would've felt like the biggest idiot ever if I slept with him, and let him got me pregnant.

Oh gosh I can't even explain how I felt after he told me that he was back with his ex-girlfriend. To tell you the truth I still feel like dirt, and used; name it that's the way I feel. Can you imagine how I would've felt if I slept with him when I decided to do so. In further ado I decided to do it with him for the first time in my life, and that's the way I got repay in humiliations.

That's how wonderful God is. He prevents me from all that; let me tell you some more about how stupid I was back in the day. Thank God who opened my eyes now; meaning I will never feel for that trick, or getting play ever again. It was a life lesson to me forever. Thank you, Lord.

So, I decided to do something so stupid like that just because I didn't want to lose what we had, and willing to break God's laws. After all that the bible says about sex before marriage, and. he humiliated me just for her. Imagine how stupid that I felt when that happened, I lost him anyway, but thank God for not letting me go through all that. In Omniscience of God; He knows what was going to happen, and took me of this mess that I was going to make for myself before my birthday.

To continue about when we went to the gym; On the way back home, he told me there is something that everyone know that you don't know. We were in 78 East that time. He told me "That there is something that everybody knows, and you didn't, and I asked him what was it? he said that I'm back with my ex-girlfriend, and he dropped me home. I went to the house all crying and stressed out let no one saw me crying, but my eyes were all red. I cried every day because of that matter, and I become so skinny like a dried stick, and decided to get baptized for real.

That experience taught me a lot of things. I seek God like I never did before, and I knew God better ever since then I never trust, or dated anyone ever again because of my first experience. Everyone asked him about our relationship, and he denied being with me all the time. I remembered when before I meant with him there was a sin that was killing me; the sin was playing with myself, and when I meant with him, he kept me so busy on the phone I never had time to do that anymore. We used to talk every second even when he was at work and I was at work our conversation was never end.

One time I left a meeting at the church on a Sunday evening just to be with him; because he called me before the meeting end to tell me that he wanted to see me. So, I left the meeting before church started at 7:30 to be with him. I remembered before I went to visit L.A we went to see a movie at the theater in Route 22: he received a text from his ex-girlfriend which happen to be his wife now, and I saw the text; it was a Thursday night.

She asked him where was he? he hides the phone from me to do not see, but I already see the message and his answered. His answered was "I'm at the rehearsal in the youth Choir in the church which was a lie, and that day I was so angry with him because of the lie. We used to go out every time he was off from his job. I was so scared because of the lie he told her. What I was thinking of is this "what if something happened to us in the road because of the lie he told?

I was so furious and scared after the movie I didn't say a word to him in our way back home. That's how much I hate lies; ever since then I didn't know if I could trust him. I questioned myself a lot about that, and he was always told me that he confused. Honestly, I didn't know nor understand why was he so confused?

And I never asked him questions about his confusions until now I understand it was because he was dating two girls at the time. Although I felt like the biggest idiot existed for trusting him for trusted him, but I thank God for him that allowed him to choose the perfect woman that God created for him; the thing is that he didn't have to lie to me about the other girls. If he told me the truth I would've just leaved what we never had alone be on my way. Now it's time for me to move on with my life.

I don't know why this nightmare has always been in my heart since 2011. I feel like the battery call Duracell. I pray all the time for God to help me put this behind me because it's not worth it to even think about. I even made a decision to not ever go back to chapter two of my book because it's too painful for me, but every time something comes to my heart, I stopped writing in this chapter before for some reason the 20th of January 2016 more stuff came to my heart to write about.

That is the only reason I wrote this as chapter one in my book. It's because this is how I found Christ. I had a dream once that I had a big book in my hand like a dictionary, so every time something came to my heart, I wrote it down in my book. Yep, this is the only reason. And again I woke up this morning, and I went to the bathroom to take a shower as I was brushing my teeth "here goes the nightmare again when I promised myself never to go back written in the second chapter of disappointment in my life; since all things are close today Sunday January 24th, 2016 after a snowstorm even churches were close. I promised God that I will spend the whole day worshiping Him, and the Holy Spirit talked to my heart by telling me to write what He told me to put in the book. He also told me that the experience I had was not all bad because it was the how God finally get my attentions.

The reason why He told me so was "I finally surrender my life to Christ Jesus because of this experience." That's why Romans 8:27-28 says that And He who searches our hearts knows the mind of the spirit, because the Spirit intercedes for God's people in accordance with the will of God. The 28 verse says that and we know that in all things God works for the good of those who love Him, have been called according to His purpose.

That's when I realized how big of a sinner I was then. Even though I came to church every Sunday back then; I was a born again Christian since Haiti to Orlando Florida and Georgia, but 2 Corinthians 5:17 was not done in my life because I didn't know the true meaning of being a newborn in Christ Jesus. The verse goes like this Therefore, if anyone is in Christ, the new creation has come; The old has gone, the new is here according to the NIV version. In John 9:1-7 Jesus healed a man born blind.

Remember what Jesus's answer to His disciples that asked Him "why the man born blind? "As you read, you'll see what Jesus answered. I believe this experience has brought me closer to Christ in many ways. That's how God really found me because I was a Sunday going church when there was more in Christ then come to heat the seat in the church while there is someone out there who wants to follow Christ, but can't come because of you occupied a place for someone. Give those who want to serve the Lord a chance to come to Jesus.

That is when I understand Matt 7:21-22 that says "Not everyone who says to me 'Lord, Lord,'will enter the kingdom of heaven, but only the one who does the will of my father who is in heaven. 22 Many will say to me on that day,; Lord, Lord, did we not prophesy in your name and your name drive out demons and in your name perform many miracles? then Jesus tells them in the 23 verse "Then I will tell them plainly, I never knew you. Away from me, you evildoers!

I was not an evildoer, but my way did not please God at all; I was one of those that were calling Jesus Lord, Lord, and was not entering to the kingdom of heaven. Like my little brother told me once if I died God would've send me straight to hell because of the things that I used to do; that did not please God. And he also told me that the reason God didn't let me die was because He didn't want to send me to hell. Thank God who didn't let me die because the way my little brother told it's like if he was Jesus, he would've sent me to hell.

My little brother condemned people like he is so Holy without sins at all; and the words of God tells us in Romans 3:23 For all have sins and fall short of the glory of God, verse 24 says and all are justified freely by His grace through the redemption that came by Christ Jesus. Maybe my little brother forgot about that verse.

In natural I called this experience a nightmare, but truly it was an opened door for me to understand Christ better; the sacrifice that Jesus was made for me by laying His body, and shedding His blood at the cross for my sins to be forgiving. Thank you, Lord Jesus Christ, for redeemed me at the cross of Calvary, and opened my Spiritual eyes to know You better. And now I understand the meaning of all my experiences in the past.

Thank God for the Holy Spirit that opened my eyes to make me see my experience in a positive way now. I used to call it many names before, but not anymore. It was supposed to be that way; that's all, and I understand it clearly now. Maybe I was crazy to think like I did before because I lacked knowledge of the Words of God when I thought that I was in a relationship, and got my heartbroken`.

As I understand now I was the only one in what I called a relationship with him, and he had his High School sweetheart. The only thing that I ask is honesty in whatever you may call it. As I was with him the girl was texting him asking him "Are you the one for me?" "And he gave me the text to read. I didn't know why he gave me the text to read, and I trusted him because I thought there was no secret between us. Because I believed in everything that he told me, that's how much I was blinded in love with him, but unfortunately, I was the only one who felt that way.

I've been playing big time because I felt for his trick, and now I feel like an idiot. Maybe I was an idiot because I never let anyone come that close to me and connected with me like that. So, he took advantage of me because I didn't have any experience in being with anybody before in my life, so I got play really well. Remembered that I explained that he told me to behave in L.A.

After I came from L.A I saw one old picture of the girl in his wallet, and I asked him; why was the picture was in his wallet? he told me it was just a picture, so I still didn't believe him. I even gave him one of my pictures from L. A, so he didn't put my picture in his wallet. One time I was talking to him in a three-way line with my girlfriend, and I explained it to my girlfriend while he was on the order line. So, my girlfriend was defended him that he can put her picture in his wallet because she was his ex-girlfriend.

Which I didn't understand why. Just because she was asking him the "is he the man for her? I told him to tell her that he had a girlfriend which was me, and he told me that he was going to tell her, but I guess he didn't tell her because he knew exactly who he loved which was her, so he stop talking to me. I lost my friend that I trusted ever since then

I'd never trust any man ever again. Imagine someone you call a friend did this to you "what would any other person do to you? It's really hard for me to trust anybody else after what I went through with him. It was strange for me, and stupid of me to let this happen to me.

I finally told my parents about our relationship when I woke up from a coma, I had those strange feelings about him to love him even more after two and a half months. Because I woke up with him in my mind to love him even more which I didn't understand, but they knew something that I didn't know. He was engaged to be married.

When I told them about my feelings for him that was when they told me that it was to late now; because he was engaged. I prayed God and asked Him "why did I felt this way for an engaged man?" I knew that the enemy was playing a game with my mind since he couldn't kill me in the accident than this. So, I rebuke the feelings because it's not possible for me to felt over him again and kept thinking of an engaged man. Writing this is not easy for me at any point, but I have to speak the truth about it.

Because it was a sin and an embarrassing moment for me, but it is a part of my testimony. What killed me the most was that a friend of mine always called me to tell me all the details that she heard, or knew about things that I didn't care about because what they were doing was not my business, and I didn't want to know about him ever again. Since God was the one who put me in the church, I couldn't leave the church because of them.

I didn't convert for anybody, so I couldn't leave the church and he did not bring me to the church; God did, and I felt like if I did that made them win. After I thought about it that way; I said to myself "You are not a coward; God has something better for, and God will lift you up right in the face of the enemies. "And a wonderful lady told me the same thing that was why I didn't live the church. Let go back to the story.

I felt so dirty, and I had my friend who introduced us at his wedding instead of helping me praying for that feeling to get away from me; he told me that I committed a sin because I had feeling, and love an engaged man is like loving a married man., The thing was that I couldn't help the way I felt for him. He killed me when he told me that first of all I didn't know about his engagement, and then it was because of the way that he told me this. It was just like if he wanted to kill me all he had to do was just to come into the nursing room where I was to poison me. He didn't have to lay it to me that way.

After that I realized some information are better to talk Jesus about because I talked to much especially about something like that. The reason why I talked to him about the strange feelings that I was having; because he alone knew about our relationship. Thank you so much my so-called friend. That is the reason why I don't have any earthly friends, but I have the best of the best friend of all; He's name is Jesus.

After losing my friend I went back to do it again. Honestly, I missed him so much; I attended a bible school; the pastor was talking to us about that particular stuff. He gave us a passage in the bible that tells us not to do such a thing. He gave us 1 Corinthians 6: 19 Do you not know that your bodies are temples of the Holy Spirit, who is in you, whom you have received from God? You are not your own; 20you were bought at a price. Therefore, honor God with your bodies. Since then, thank God when I knew what the words of God says about sex before marriage, and what my body was I stopped doing.

I hated it that I never do it again after knowing the truth about it; thank God I never go that far with him no matter what. And I believe one thing he was not the one for. Thank God he found the woman that God has for him, and now they are happily married "glory to God for them". The title of this is "The Loved of My Life" which I used a past tense for love because it was my past experience". I know better that God will send me the right man if it's in His Will.

Can you believe that after where God took me from an accident, I went back to do that disgusting thing? I cried and asked God to purified me because I'm not worthy for His grace. That's why I asked God to please send me the husband that He created for me because I couldn't deal with my flesh anymore. I even asked God to take away my flesh desires from me because I was at a point it became too much for me. I prayed for God to forgive me when I did it, but that wasn't enough.

I just didn't want to feel like that anymore because it got to a point where it was killing me. And I asked about the prayer that I made because it came even more than when they told me that; it's normal for me to feel that way because God created me with them. There are some prayers that God will never answer, and ever since then I stop making those prayers.

I cried when it came, and ask God to calm it down for me until He send me the significant one because I was so tired. I am being honest because as human we have that special need one time or another; one thing to know that to cry out to God to strengthen you, and to rebuke the devil. It is normal to feel that way.

Just because it's normal doesn't mean that you have acted on it. Just pray to God to send you the significant one. Don't just go look for him because you can find yourself in the bigger mess. I know that because I went through it myself. I didn't even look for it, and it found me therefore I felt for it. Don't make the same mistake that I made. Trust God and stay in prayer. I arrived at a time when I said to myself that I didn't want anybody in my life ever again, because I was so disappointed before and I thought that I could live my life by myself.

I only said that because my first relationship was so hurt in it that I didn't even know what it was. What I thought it was; wasn't that at all. Women out there the man that God has for you will find you do not go look for him, so let him find you. Don't let age make you do something that you will regret all your life, and deceive you. God has a man for every one of you. Just wait on Him because His time is the best time. My point in telling you this story is that my life was not always perfect as it seems to be.

Before I met Christ Jesus; I used to be a trash can. And when I met Him; He washed me clean with His blood to change my life, and put His Holy Spirit in me. I called myself a trash can because I used to do all these bad things before, I knew Christ. But 1 John 1:9 says If we confess our sins, He is faithful and just and will forgive us our sins and purify us from all unrighteousness. It doesn't matter that anyone who read my story condemned me for my pass.

I know one thing that God has forgiven me already, and Romans 8:1 says that therefore, there is no condemnation for those who are in Christ Jesus,2 through Christ Jesus the law of the spirit who gives life has set me free from the law of sin and death. Somebody like me is not worthy of the forgiveness of Christ Jesus; after all these bad things that I used to do, because I didn't know Jesus like I know him now, and I confess it to the whole wild world how I used to be.

For doing this doesn't make me a pervert, but in honest soul. The thing is I don't care what anybody think of me right now "the past is the past, so nothing I can do nor changed about it; because it's really happened and I can't change the pass mistake that I made." Only one thing that I know that I can have better future with Christ Jesus.

I know that in Isaiah 43:18-19 says: Forget the former things; do not dwell on the past.19 See, I am doing a new thing! Now it springs up; do you not perceive it? I am making a way in the wilderness and streams in the wasteland. I am supposed to keep dwelling in the past, but I made a lot of mistakes in the past I also believe that God has a bright future for me.

I learned a valuable lessons from my past experiences in order for me to share it with you guys; because I understand it when somebody is going through the same thing that I went through in order for me to give them advice. It's not easy believe me I know. But all things that happened to our lives has a purpose or a reason, and the reason is not to kill you, but to prepare you.

The reason why I share this with you is because it's not good to do; I'd been through it before, and I didn't like it at all. It doesn't satisfy your need like having a partner would; it only lasts for a few second, I mean the inch, but that inch can bring you to hell if Jesus comes, and found you're doing it. Remember what the bible says about the second coming of Jesus; He will come like a thief at night to be clear about what I just tell you guys I will give you a verse that describes it.

Matthew 24:42-44 "Therefore keep watch, because you do not know on what day your Lord will come.43 But understand this: if the owner of the house had known at what time of night the thief was coming, he would not have let his house be broken into.44 So you also must be ready, because the Son of Man will come at an hour when you do not expect Him. Be careful on what you're doing. These few seconds can cost you an eternal life to hell fire. Think about it; do not let your flesh deceive you. It's not worth it to go to an eternal fire that's never going to stop, and you will never die.

Your friends will be Satan and worms; nobody want that where you're going to be burn in a fire that's never going to switch off, and you're never going to die in it. All is there is suffering like you haven't been suffering enough in this earth. Please think about it; just like I rebuked it and cried out to God for help, and He help me with the situation. I believe that God can, and is able to help you just like He did for me. God didn't created hell for us to go into, but for the devil and his angels.

The devil is looking to bring you with him, so don't let him trick you to go with him there. Remember sin is not ugly; it's the sweetest thing ever, and can destroy you in a few second you feel the flesh desire, and if you act on it. As for me the devil is a liar, and is not bringing me with him to the pit of fire that's reserved for him. I am victorious from that thing forever and ever. Praise God! thank you Jesus for setting me free from all that. I love you Jesus.

May the Will of God be done in my life because my life is not my own anymore to God I belong. I remembered as I went to shower, and how I didn't feel like writing two pages of essays when I was in college, and now I am writing a book. That make me Praise God more for His awesomeness, because back in the day when my teachers gave me essays to do I always go for help from a smart friend to help me with it. I had my ex-friend who so smart in that level, and a type fast as well every time I had an essay, he was the first person that I had in mind to call, and ask for help, and he always so nice to help, and end up doing all the work for me.

Remember what I wrote in my previous chapter of my book; I was dead, and God gave me His life to live, and I believed it too that's why I need to live that life as God wants me too. Because I'm not just come to church because everyone is going. In the book of Matthew 7:21 says that "Not everyone who says to me 'Lord, Lord, will enter the Kingdom of Heaven, but the one who does the will of my Father who is in heaven.

That verse makes me understand to do not come call yourself believers, and just come to please somebody that make our flesh inch when seeing that person going to church, and feel like we have to make our neighbor see that we are church material as well.

Don't come church to fool anybody, or think that we could fool God. What I would say about that you can fool people, but not God because God knows our just before we made the action. Like I said God came from too far with me to come as an imposter in the Gospel. I'm still young I can wait for God Will to be done in my life. As for me I said that if God sent me to this earth to have a family on my own may the Will of God be done in my life. As for me I am not going to look for anybody to break my heart again.

Girls that read this I have one advice for all of you "Do not let your flesh deceive you. "When you can't handle it anymore go to God in prayer in order for Him to give you the one that He created for you. Don't do what I did to choose any man just because your flesh is to much for you. In God time you will find the right man. Not in your time; in God time, because God time is the best time. Remember in the previous paragraph I mentioned the mystery man Melchizedek "who was He? According to my research the hint that I found is that Notice that Melchizedek was King of Salem; Salem is a city of Jerusalem. Salem comes from the Hebrew word meaning "peace. "That would make Melchizedek the "King of Peace "according to Hebrew 7:2. The Hebrew name Melchizedek itself means; King of Righteousness Hebrew 7:2. The same individual is mentioned in Psalm 110:4. Speaking prophetically of Christ, David stated: The Eternal hath sworn, and will not repent, Thou art a priest forever after the order of Melchizedek. This verse is quoted again in Hebrews 5:6,10.

For this Melchizedek of Salem, priest of the Highest God. Since God names individuals what they are that, then is what this man is. "King of Righteousness. Think of it! King of Righteousness. Jesus Himself said: There is none good but one, that is God (Matthew 19:17) Human self -righteousness is, before God, as filthy rags. None can be righteous but God -or one made righteous by God's power -Christ in a person! And certainly, none but One of the Godhead the divine Kingdom of God would be King of Righteousness.

Such an expression, applied to any but God, would be blasphemous. Thinking about it is so clear that God Himself came to be among us and tried to understand what those verses are trying to tell us about Him according to Genesis 14:18-20, and Hebrew 7. No man is righteous, but God Himself.

Don't trust yourself because you don't know yourself like God knows you. He has the perfect plan in everyone's life. Remember what Jeremiah 29:11 says. Always think that your life is not your own. The owner of your life has control if you let Him. God bless you all. I woke up in a dream in the 9th of December; I don't know the meaning of it, but God knows.

I will talk more about it when God gives me a confirmation of it, and you will understand. This morning December 10th of 2015 I also had a revelation from God about whom Melchizedek was, and I went to the bible in Genesis 14:18-20, and Hebrews 7 where they mentioned His name "who He was, and who He is. The book of Genesis and the book of Hebrew are the two books that they mentioned Him.

I am more than happy to share it with you if you have any question about it feel free to ask me. It is all in my testimony that is why I mention it to chapter two of my book "My First love, But Not My Last. "God bless you all. Have Faith, and God will do something greater in your life that you can't even imagine; just like I believe that He will deliver me from that nightmare.

He's able to do it for me and for you as well. My birthday is coming very soon next week by the 30th of December 2015 when I was supposed to die two years ago. What the doctors says it's not what God says because the doctors gave me 10% chance to wake up from coma, I was going to be only 27 years old then, and now I'm going to be 29. Isn't God great? Psalms 46:10 says Be still, and know that I am God; I will be exalted among the nations, I will be exalted in the earth.

What I mean to say is that God have the final say for my life, and I will serve the Lord with all my life. Because He deserves it not only,

He saves me from myself; from being a major mess as a masturbator in the past, and now He add even more years in my life after dying in the hospital bed in August 27, 2013. I will give you youngsters an advice that a wise woman gave me once. She told me to say this prayer "God please do not let the enemy know my weakness because he always seats at your weakness in order to use it against you."

Once he knows your weaknesses you are in big trouble, and I said that prayer God made me overcome the process that I was going through from that advice." Thank you, mommy, and I love you so much because you have been the mother that I never had when I was growing up; because if you were in my life when I was younger there are some mistakes that I would've never made in my life. I thank God for you being in my life, and for God to add more and more years to your life in order for the grandchildren that God will give you by me not to go through the same thing that I went to because they will have you as the best grandma ever.

You know who you are my wonderful mommy therefore I do not have to mention your name in this chapter. I love you mommy T.B, and may God bless you abundantly. I believe that God put you in my life for a reason. You always tell me not to worry about the past because God has a greater and a brighter future for me. Speaking of the mother that I never had, and now I realize something greater about our relationship.

By that I mean that you are really my mother, because you had us twins in your womb you didn't know. After giving birth to me you were still in pain, so you gave birth to my 18 days old younger twin brother. Since we did not grow up together; each of us grew up with a different family which is your family also when we met and we got connected again, and end up dating unfortunately you didn't know about it we had kept our relationship as secret from you and my other family. That was the reason why we have different last name.

You heard about Fairy Tales; it's just a story not necessarily truth, so think of my story as a Fairy Tale as you read it. I'm not asking you guys to believe it, but understand the meaning of the love that is in the story. The love of a mother for her child is the love that my mommy shows me every day. Especially after my accident she is the only one that keeps me from feeling neglected. She always calls me, and supports me that's the kind of love that I'm talking about.

I got my heartbroken by my twin brother I'm not going to mention my twin brother's name because this chapter of my life is over years ago; I can never hate my twin brother for what happened only one thing I do know that God has a reason or a purpose for everything that happens in each and everyone's life.

People that are reading my book; you need to know that I did not know that we were related when I had my heart broken by him and the story comes alive. Hurts but good, and I got connected more with my mommy not with my twin brother because we are not friends after what happened, but he is still my brother. I have no choice but to love him even though we are not friends anymore. I love that woman just like she raised me.

I love your faith mommy; your faith is greater than mine; when I thought that everything was over in my life you always boost me up to make me believe again all is not over; it's just the beginning. You always use by God to give me some wonderful advice that I don't get from anybody else because I do not trust most of the people that I talk to. In order for me to take advice from anyone; I have to see what is your relationship with God is. I see something from you that I don't find in anybody else.

You are an angel from above to me because you're always have the best advice for me even when I don't even tell you about what I'm going through, but you're always come straight to what I'm going for some reason. Just like when somebody is going through something, and open the Bible open it in the passage that talks according to the situation that (he or she is going through) Hallelujah! Praise God.

He alone could do that. Thank you, Lord. I arrived in a point the 24th of December, 2015, Christmas Eve felt so tired of chapter two of my book, and I prayed with tears in my eyes "God you knew what I've been through in my past, and I don't want to think about it anymore nor to write about it, so please open a new chapter in my life in Jesus mighty name; and I believed that you're going to it for me please close the chapter of my life because you said in Isaiah 43:18-19 to "Forget the former things; do not dwell on the past. I'm doing a new thing! Now it springs up; do you not perceive it. Yeah, I repeat that verse again Isaiah 43:18-19.

The reason why I prayed that prayer was because I was tired of living in the past. It brought the pains over and over again to my life. In other words, it was too painful for me to bare. I thank God for the strength that He gives me because in my experience I believe that God didn't give me more than I could handle. So, I believe in the new chapter that God is going to add in my life. I don't know if it's going to be the last chapter which I hope not because I believe that God has more blessings stored for me. I have faith that it's not over. In Hebrews 11:1 says that "Now faith is confidence in what we hope for and assurance about what we do not see." God help me, please only You can.

Why Am I Still Hurt Over a Nonsense?

Imagine that happened in 2010. My heart is till bleeding, and I don't understand why? It's been seven years since I got my heartbroken by my former best friend, and that pain is still in my heart. I prayed for God to help me to move on with my life, but for some reason it's not easy. They 'are people that claimed to be servants of God that I shared my story with because I trusted them. It was the biggest mistake that I made for trusting them. The reason why was because after talking to them; they went to judge me. I didn't have control over my feelings if I didn't understand what was going on; I would've stopped if I could. Could you imagine after all these years this player is still in my mind. I fastened for God to help me forget about his existence of never him, but nothing works. I believe God will send me my prince someday, and I will forget that I never knew someone like that. My family is pressuring me on getting a man, but I am not looking for a man to have kids with, but I waiting for the one that God created for me. Who would not hurt me, but support me, and love even with my disability?

I cried every day when people are not around. I couldn't bare the tears that I have deep in my heart, and in my eyes. When I feel like crying "I sing, I praise God because only God could ease my tears. At night I cry on my pillow where nobody could hear me. I have my radio on at all time, so my family to do not hear me crying. If pillow could've talk mine would've. I needed someone to talk to when mankind is judging me; I learned to turn to God with my problems. God is the only one that understand my pain therefore I stopped talking to people about my problems. Sometimes I am cheerful, and sometimes I'm not. I tried to always put a smile on my face even when I'm sad. I don't like when people are asking me questions when I have a long face.

When they ask me "what's wrong" it makes me want to cry, and I couldn't do that in front of those judges. Those judges are there just to judge, and shame on me that always give them a reason to judge me. They don't understand me, and I don't expect for them to understand me either. I'm afraid of putting myself out there because I said that I am done with this thing. I don't want to hurt myself anymore, and I'm tired of it. It comes to a point where I am tired of hurting myself over something that was never there. The reality is right in front of me instead of facing it I want to run away from it. The person moved on with his life, and I'm hurting mine. If God gives me permission to move out of New Jersey I would. I want to move somewhere far from New Jersey maybe go back to Florida to start over with my life. It's hard for me at all points; that's why I want to run far away from where I would never see him again, but the Lord says No. Wherever I'll be I don't want anybody to come close to me to break my heart again. In fact, I think I'm done with that thing. Sometime what we say; it's not what God say, and I know that God has a big plan for my life. I prayed a lot for God to give me a lot of patience to wait on His time because God time is the best.

I'll stay away from men that's why I ask God for a sign when the right one come in other for me not to scare him away. I don't trust myself to choose anyone anymore. What I called love failed because it didn't have a foundation. "Psalms 127:1 Unless the Lord builds the house, those who build it labor in vain. Unless the Lord watches over the city, the watchman stays awake in vain." I thought what I had was love because it seems like it, but in reality, it was not. The reason why I' use this verse is because I didn't put God first in it; in consequences I'm hurting myself over in over again. I don't have to blame anyone but myself. I should've known better to trust in Lord instead of trusting God; I found myself in that big mess. All I need is for my heart to be whole again. I don't understand why that thing is still bothering my spirit, and I let it to put tears in my eyes every times. God, please hear my prayers because I'm tired of this nonsense.

I Prayer for My Heart to be healing.

"My tears are still their O Lord, please wipe away my tears for me. It has been forever, and I want to be over this pain. I remembered when I used to cry a lot back in 2015; You sent me to read John 16 which I still read when the pain come, and my tears were dried. Please help me Lord to forget if I ever experienced this. I am not a Duracell battery that last for a long time, and I am so tired of this pain. You did it once, and I trust in You O Lord in due time to heal my heart again. I don't understand why this still there. Please Lord help on that journey; heal because my heart for your glory. I want to get over this, and only You could help me. I'm waiting on you my Lord, my healer, my protector; you healed me physically already, and now I want my heart to be healed in Jesus' name." Amen. After all, I was seeking God just like Isaiah 55:6 say "⁶ Seek ye the LORD while he may be found, call ye upon him while he is near:" While I was seeking for God, that happened to me.

"The Testimony of My Life"

At twenty-six years old, after my heart break while I was seeking on the Lord, I went from size ten to a size four. I was depressed, and confused. I was in a fast without knowing. I lead a youth service on Monday night, and everyone was talking about the service, and the next day Tuesday, I was struck by a car, and I woke up in the hospital from coma after three months. I was a TBI patient because I was injured more in my head. The right side of my head; the skull and spent 5 months out in laboratory all the way to China, and in January 31,2014 the doctor put them back. I can say that the world was praying for me, and God restored me completely.

Specially to give you guys an idea of what God can do because the nature of God never changed. In Hebrews 13:8 Jesus Christ is the same yesterday and today and forever.

When you're looking at me right now, and see my accident pictures you will understand what I mean by that verse. In my experience with God; I believe that I was in God's University, and I had to go through trials in my life. The Christian life doesn't mean everything will be smooth all the way because Jesus even told that in (John 16:33) "I have told you these things, so that in me you may have peace. In this world you will have trouble. But take heart! I have overcome the world.". That's why I never discouraged because James 1:2-4 says that the trials are not here to kill us, but to test our faith to make us grow stronger in Christ Jesus.

The trials gave me the strength, because every time the trials came to my life, I said to myself "it is all in God's plan." Because I know that God has a plan in my life, and God brought me back to life for a reason. When doctors gave me 10% chance to wake up in the coma, I was for three months because I was young, and the doctor called my spiritual mother aside to tell her that I was dead, so he just didn't know how to tell my father.

They thought that I was crazy even the house manager thought that. I said that I didn't care of what anybody thinks because God knows it all how they've been treated me. So, the staff yelled at me, and I screamed back because I felt like at my age (29) years old nobody has the right to treat me as such, or to scream at me because I am not their child. I also know that they wrote me up just because I could not stand at getting yell at. I knows that just because I was a TBI (Traumatic Brain Injury) patient that didn't them the reason why to treat me like they did, and I didn't like the way they treated me at all.

They have good therapy over there. I came to the group home with a walker after three, or four months I was discharged from the walker to a cane.

After two months with the cane, I got discharged from it as well. God delivered me from all these objects, and now God has me walking on my own. That's how amazing our God is. I only went to the group home because of my brain injury. That's why my father chose the group home for me, and my father didn't have a place to put me. I was discharged from therapy, I had my driver's license, and want to be independent like I used to be before my accident. I had to have an EEG test for the doctor to check if I still have seizure in my system; thank God everything is ok. They don't find any trace of seizure. God is good.

I was encouraged by people who love me to write a book about my life testimony that God gave me. To be shared with all of the people from all over the World just to encourage them to seek God even in the difficulties. God can do the same things that He does for me for everyone who trust, and believe in Him. I also asked God to guide me, and to deliver me from myself. For some reason one morning I went to take a shower it came to my heart to start the fourth chapter in my book, and the voice told me to write about the keys to a successful marriage and I did.

I believe in Lamentations 3:26 that talk about "It is good to wait quietly for the salvation of the Lord." Sometimes God made a complete silence in the situations that we are in because He has a final say in the situation, and when He kept silent like that when He has to talk deliverance come. When God doesn't say anything in your situations that doesn't mean He doesn't care; all we have to do is to have patient and wait for Him.

Since I'm not yet married, I trusted the voice to dictate to me what to write, and It gave me what to write although it has nothing to do with my testimony. What I didn't understand was that my first so call relationship, failed because I didn't anything about how to be in a relationship, and now I'm the one to write about the keys for a successful marriage. God is good I hope that in my marriage I apply all the keys that I was given, and have given to you guys married and future married folks. Because I wasn't so good at dating enjoy the book. God bless you all. Good lecture.

The Scenario

⬦◈⬦

I came from my country at seventeen years old, and I used to live in Orlando Florida for 3 years. My dad moved to Georgia in January 2007, and he sent me to New Jersey to live with my aunt in March 10,2007. In August 27,2013 I went to fasting on that Tuesday morning, and I got hit by a car later in the afternoon. I was only 26 going to 27 years old in December in the same year of 2013, and the accident was so terrible. I was dead God saved my life. God rose me from the death just like He did for Lazarus. God is so good; He add many more years to my life. Now it has been ten years and I'm still alive. Thanks to the almighty.

I was supposed to be dead since August,2013, and God said in "Psalms 46:10 Be still, and know that I am God. I will be exalted among the nations; I will be exalted in the earth!11 The Lord of hosts is with me; and the God of Jacob is my fortress. In God plan it wasn't the time for me to die. He gives me life to live again. Praise His Holy name. I used to go to church 7 days a week.

My family thought that I was lazy because I never stay in the house. What they didn't know was that I was seeking God just like Isaiah 55:6 says "Seek the Lord while He may be found; call upon Him while He is near." They didn't understand me, and what I was going through at all because I didn't get a chance to tell them what I was going through. Remember I was in a so-called relationship they didn't know about. Even if they knew what I was going through; there is nothing that they could've done for me. I lost my job since 2011 I was stressing and couldn't concentrate; something that I could only talk to God about.

I was constantly in church because in Matthew 6:31-33 says that "So do not worry, saying, what shall we eat? "Or What shall we drink? or what shall we wear?32 For the pagans run after all these things, and your heavenly Father knows that you need them.33 But seek first His kingdom and His righteousness, and all these things will be given to you as well. So, while I was going to church, I went to school as well, and I applied for job they never called me "not even one" so my dear cousin was paying my phone bills for me. Only God knows what I was going through, and understand me too. For God to understand our pain He came himself in flesh.

He was tempted, and hungry too. That's why I said that only Him knows what I was going through stuff that I couldn't talk to anyone about God was the only one that I trusted with my personal life, because He knows, and understand me always. One time my dad came to pick me up at the group home for church, and he told me that whenever a man come to ask him for my hand of marriage, he will make sure to let him know in advance that I don't like to work.

I didn't say anything to him because he did not understand. My aunt told me once "now I see why you were always in church "she said that because she saw when I had the accident all churches that I used to go to stand in the hospital praying for me. They were always come to see me in the hospital. Don't be discourage to seek God. You are not going to regret it.

I started to write the testimony of my life testimony. God is too good in my life I cannot just not saying anything about how great is my God is. Like John 3:16 says, For God so loved the World that He gave His only begotten Son, that whoever believed in Him should not perish, but have everlasting life. In August 27, 2013 I got hit by a car ever since then I woke up in the hospital thinking that I went to pray with somebody.

I found myself surrounded with my friends, and I asked them "who did we come to pray with today?" And they told me "No, you didn't come to pray with anybody, it's you that we came to see". I still didn't understand what they were talking about. I was in coma for 2 in a half month. I didn't know anybody then. They told me everything that happened, how I was hit by a car that an old lady who was 82 years old driving. Thank God that saved my life. I woke up in a wheelchair. When I had my last surgery, I end up to the nursing home with the wheelchair. Since they didn't give me therapy there, I took a walker that a friend gave to my aunt for me, and started to walk with it.

God took the wheelchair away from me I never knew where the wheelchair went, so I continued with my walker since then, and I went to the group home with my walker. Every time I went to therapy, I always brought my walker with me. After three or four months I was discharged from it, and they gave me a cane to walk with. After two to three months, I was discharged from the cane as well. God took all those objects from me within a year.

That's what God can do, and He deserves all the thanks, and the glory. In August 2015 God sent me to Haiti for the first time since September 2004. I was so happy visit my country again, I saw people that I knew before I came to the United States of America when I called them by their name, they didn't know who I was.

That's when I told them who my mother and father was 'they were surprised, and said to me we thought you buried already" I answered them nicely "God resurrected me "Jesus did it. The reason why they thought that I was dead it was because that was the news, they received that I had an accident, and I was dead. I told them Jesus is the resurrection and the Life He breath life in me, I went to give a Thanksgiving to God for Who He is, and what He has done that made people surprised.

I know when you're giving thanks to God you are not supposed to ask Him for anything, but I asked Him for one thing that I needed most "Just for Him to come and take His thanks", and He came that made me so happy because I felt the presence of God just like I asked.

Just like Matthew 7:7 says "Ask and it will be given to you; seek and you will find; knock and the door will be opened to you. Hallelujah! And I got just what I asked God for. Thank You, God, for answering my prayers, and I know that You will answer all my prayers in Your own time because You fix one day for everything in my life. I love you Lord with all my life which I always tell people "The life that I'm living now it's not my own; it is Jesus's Life that I'm living "which mean that I can't do what I want with that life.

May the Will of God be done through my life. I'm done with the flesh desires because in "Galatians 5;16 says that, So I say, walk by the Spirit, and will not gratify the desires of the flesh.17 For the flesh desires what is contrary to the Spirit, and the Spirit what is contrary to the flesh. They are in conflict with each other, so that you are not to do whatever you want.

My father told me that they had to teach me how to speak again in Speech Therapy. I had to learn Kindergarten stuff over and over again like math 1+1= 2, A, B, C all over again. I didn't know any of those time when these happened to me, the only thing I remembered is when I was in Speech Therapy. Like I said had tubs all over my body; One in my neck to help me breath, one to help me pee, one to feed me, the one to feed me was also to flush every time to help me drink water, and the porridge as food because I couldn't swallow, or taste anything through my mouth because I couldn't chew anything in my mouth.

I was in thickness drinks and food I can say that the 27 years old girl became a newborn baby again all over, and now I shower by myself, dressing, and feeding by myself that's how awesome Go is people. God make the impossible in my life become possible that's the Almighty God that I serve. God is Omnipotent, Omnipresent, and Omniscient.

In His Omnipotent; meaning He is all Powerful, in His Omnipresent; meaning He is everywhere, and His Omniscient meaning He knows everything. He so powerful to saved my life in the accident, and He was there to push me away from the tires of the car when the car hit me, and He knows that was going to happen before it happened.

He could've avoided me from getting by the car, but for His glory He let it happened in order for me to have the experience that Job had with Him "when Job had the experience with Him everyone was telling Job to denied that God that let this to happen to him, and his answered was in Job 1:21 And he said, Naked I came from my mother's womb, and naked shall I return. The Lord gave, and the Lord has taken away; blessed be the name of the Lord.

And in John 9 when the disciples asked Jesus why the young man born blind "was it the sins of his mother, father that caused his blindness? Remember what Jesus answered them in John 9:3 Neither this man nor his parents sinned, 'Jesus said, but this happened so that the works of God might be displayed in him. Jesus made the young man sees. God let things happen to us because He knows how to deliver us through them. Don't ask Him" why" instead ask Him what He wants you do for Him. It was my trials that I had to get to the destination that God want to bring me.

God is the same yesterday, today, and forever more. Honestly the things that I've been told that happened to me was the same things I read in the bible. God saved the three young Hebrews from a burning fiery furnace, and Daniel in the pit of lions, Rose Lazarus from death, and He also rose me from the death. I was so dead doctors gave my dad 10%chance for me to wake up from the coma, and he told my spiritual mother that I was dead, but didn't know how to tell my dad because my dad was suffered already.

The thing is when they were explaining all the story to me. I told them what the doctors don't know that my God is the Resurrection and the Life, and God has the last saying of everyone's life. Doctors can give chances, but God breathe life into me. Praise God. I used the verse of Psalms 34" I will bless the Lord at all times; His praise shall continually be in my mouth."

This morning I wake up more thought come to my mind about what happened to me. In all the experiences that I was in. All churches were in prayer for me even some of them didn't even know me. Some of them even fast for me as well. Everyone was in their knees for me. That time my spiritual mother went in mission she went there for a different cause, and she put my name in the mission as well therefore everybody was praying for me.

Thank you, my mommy, for loving me so much, and love you as well. May God bless abundantly your ministry, and your family. Thank you all from House of Prayer that always came to support me in the hospital, and pray for me in the Rehab center. I had the most wonderful time of my life.

The people that work there were so nice, and supportive. I had the best therapist ever; Physical, Occupational, Speech, and Cognitive therapy over there. There are no better place the than the rehab at Kessler Institute in Saddle Brook. I was there for months compared to the order place that I had rehab; they're the best. They treated me like a princess over there. I remembered when I was turning twenty-seven, they threw a surprise party for me including friends and family. This is an experience that I would never forget; the cognitive therapist made a beautiful shirt for me that said; Happy Birthday princess. It was design so beautifully, and I was speechless that's how happy I was.

I miss them so much I wish to pay them a visit sometimes in the future to show them my gratitude toward them. How I appreciated them, and I miss my first physical therapist (PT) that I had; she moved to P.A. Every time she comes to visit NJ, she always pays me a visit at the group home where I was, and every Christmas she always sends me a card to show me how much she misses me. She told me in the card that she always thinks about me. That shows me how much she cares about me, and how much she appreciates me. I love you as well Suzie. After all I miss everyone.

I really miss you guys. I know that I'm not supposed to mention any name in my book, but you are exceptional to me. I came from Kessler at midnight January 30,2014 for my last surgery to have my skull put back in my head. In December 19,2015 I went back to visit them; everybody showed me the same worm love that they gave me a year ago. I felt so loved around them, and I went to get Suzie number personally to give her a call. Every year on my birthday she sends me a birthday card. Isn't she sweet?

All my therapists from the rehab, and the others as well. I remember a joke that my speech therapy thought me; every time that joke come to my mind, I laugh so much I started to give the joke at the group home that I was in they laughed as well because it was so funny.

I was so happy to have her number again, and to hear her voice again; also, to have my old speech therapist Samantha's number as well, and hear both of their voices again. I was so happy to have their contacts back. I used to love singing Celine Dion when I was there; she bought Celine Dion products for my 27th birthday, and I was so happy.

When I talked to her, and told her that I was writing a book about the testimony of my life; she was so excited for me, and she told me that she cannot wait to read my book. That's the kind of love I've been telling you about even the nurses and the staff was so happy to see the progress that I have made since I was discharged, and how God work His miracles in my life. I'm so happy to hear wonderful news about my fellow therapist; all of them are married, and have kids. Isn't this wonderful?

I really appreciate your support toward me. May God bless you abundantly with all kind of blessing. I love everybody that took good care of me when I was there God bless all of you. I miss you guys as well. You made me feel like a princess when I was there seriously. The birthday party that you guys collaborated with my family, and friends to throw me was the first time in my life I had a party like for my birthday, and I enjoyed every minutes of it. Suzie even physically you were not there, but spiritually you were there. I received your gift, and I appreciated. And as for you my brothers, sister's therapist who showed me your love, and your participations I really appreciate you guys as well. I wish I didn't have to leave so soon.

There is no way I could compare the love that you guys showed me with anything; you didn't even know me like that, but you loved me like somebody you knew for a long time. Thank you, guys, and I remembered one the nurses who took care of me said to me "You need to write a book about your testimony" I laughed when she told me so, and to confirm what she told me mommy told me the same thing. I started writing the book about what God has done in my life.

God bless you all that God used to take good care of me when I was with you guys, and thank you Dr Averill for being there for me when I was crying like a baby. You understood my pain you treated me just like your daughter. I will never forget you guys, and I promise that to give you a visit as soon as I get a chance.

In fact, I thank everyone who was in praying for me, and first I thank God for everything. God take all the pain for me. As you can see God answer all of your prayers. I had four surgeries in my head, and I had a stroke because of too much pain that I was in. I'm done with all my therapy. You see how our God works in mysterious way. When my spiritual mother heard that she put her ministry in fasting and prayers for me. God answered their prayers, and restored my soul. I also believed that "the same God that started with me will finished what's He began with in my life." Because God always finishes His work. I also said that God didn't create me as a disabled person which a lot of people made me uncomfortable when they're treating her as such. I explained to the bosses how the I was being treated by all rehabilitations that she was in which I didn't like at all. When you read the body paragraph in the book you will have an idea of what it was for me.

Some of the people who recognized me before they can't believe How I look today because God change me completely. Before I was a skinny girl, and know my complexion changed when they see me now, they barely recognized me now. I'm going to use a French word "Jesus is the repairer of breaches, He restores me." I really appreciate all of you my family in Christ Jesus, my biological family as well. I thank God for all of you especially for my dad that God strengthen to deal with all of it.

I heard that my dad, and my aunt always spent the night at the hospital without food, nor sleep just to represent me in the hospital for when the doctors came, and asked for my family they were always there. I didn't know that my family love me like that. I love you guys as well, and thank for doing this for me.

Mommy always called me till now just to make sure that I'm ok, and how am I doing? She prayed with me, and give me good advice as always. "I could say that she is an Angel from heaven sent by God to me. God bless you my wonderful mommy in Christ Jesus.

God bless you dad. And they also told me that my dad, and my aunt called out in their job to take care of me. Some people thought that my aunt was my mom because she always took over to send my dad to get something to eat, and to get some rest. I'm so thankful for you guys. God bless you dad and aunty. I have a reason to always tell my story to the wide World. As I was about to take a shower I was thinking more about my life. I remembered that I was at Kessler for months after the accident, and I started to remember every face that came to see me. I had a very high fever on me which gave a stroke.

My dad asked the doctor why did I had the stroke, and the doctor told him that I was in so much pain that's the reason I had the stroke. That stroke took all my right side which made all my right side weak, and my right hand was close under my chin. I couldn't opened it at all in order for me to get feed the doctor put a G-tube in my stomach. I remember when the doctor took the G-tub out, I didn't feel any pain at all. It was healed in a week, Jesus took all the pains for me at the cross. I had five surgery in my head, and one in my arm because my left bone was crushed by the tire of the car, therefore the bone was replaced by a metal.

I remembered when I was in the nursing home for the first time, I felt my left arm that have the metal was hurting me, and I prayed God to help me with that strange feeling in my arm. I said; Jesus' The Doctor by excellence when I was in the Nursing home, I felt a pain on my left shoulder where I have a metal on that I never felt before, so the bible in Isaiah 53: 5 tells me that by your stripes that I am healed. I believe it, and I know and believe there is power in your blood please make that pain go away for me. I prayed with the Words of God, As I applied the blood of Jesus on it, I never felt that pain ever again. Glory to God in the Highest Place.

I was an adult in diaper because I couldn't do anything by myself in order for me to pee, or to do the number two I had to do it all in my diaper. People came to pray with me every day. I didn't know that I was well known by a lot of people like that which remind me that only in Christ Jesus you have a lot of family. And I realized my true family is in Christ Jesus. I used to go to church seven days a week. I was in all the prayers that make me miss church a lot when church is working, I can't attend it. I had five surgeries in my head.

The last surgery that I had in my right side of my head because when I woke up, I didn't have my right skull and brain because my accident was so tragic the doctor had to send them all the way to China for six months. In 31 of January 2014, they had to put them back.

The insurance didn't want to pay for it, but God did it before human doctors can even touch my head. I had a dream that 3 people took me to a room, and put me in a bed started doing a supernatural surgery for me. Since the insurance didn't want to pay for my last head surgery for me God did it, and they were a Thanksgiving in House of Prayer I called them to explain the dream, and also to participate in the Thanksgiving as well.

As I was explaining the dream to them my aunt told me on the phone that the insurance sent them a letter that say they agreed to pay for the surgery for me. You see how God works. God works in mysterious way that we human could never understand. We can never understand God way just believe, and have faith because with God anything is possible 'like Hebrews 11:1 says that Faith is the assurance of things hoped for, the conviction of things not seen.'

God is so good I can talk nonstop about the gracious of God. I was dead, and He rose me from the death as I explained earlier. After my last surgery they put me in a Nursing home for 5 months I felt so alone most of the times because I didn't have anyone to talk to. As I was in the Nursing home, they didn't give me any therapy at all because my insurance didn't cover therapy for me, but a friend gave my aunt a walker for me I tried to walk with the walker every day because there was a time, I never see my wheelchair anymore because God took it away.

When I used to walk with my walker alone like that people that are working in the Nursing home was so panic for me because they were scared that I could felt. I told them "Do not be scared because I'm not alone". I also have the anointing of God on me. What God has plan for that new life that He gives me will come to pass because when I was in the nursing home every time, I was working with my walker there is nurse that always gave me my medicine when I passed by her, she always had goosebumps, and she always told me that she didn't understand why is that always happened. One day she came to give me the meds, and she end up praying for me.

As she was praying her tongue change, and she told me that God put something really special inside of me. Always do what God ask me to do. Just obey to God, and I answered her that I will always obey God's voice when He talk to me, and she left. The reason why I told them that I wasn't alone was because I remember the first time, I took my walker to walk by myself because I felt so alone so sad most of the time, and as I was walking sad and lonely, I heard the voice of God that told me "Daughter you are not alone.

I command my angels to be with you, and to guide you" That morning I got a strength that came onto me ever since then I walked every day when they got panic I always told them that I'm not alone in order for them to give a break. I was in the room 12. One time at the nursing home, as I laid in the bed that they put me on I heard a voice that told me to raise my right hand up for the first time I listened to the voice, and I did remember when I told you my right hand was closed under my chin, but that day.

As I tried to raise it up like the voice told me to my tongue changed instantly, and my hand that was under my chin was opened praise God. God is good at all time. This is not just a story it is a life testimony everybody who saw me before could testify about it. Everyone who came to see me in the hospital was so scared, and started crying because of the condition that I was in.

Some of them didn't see life in me at all not even the doctors because they told my dad that I had 10% chance to wake up in the coma that I was in, but Jesus' breath His life in me gives a brand-new life to live. That's why I said the life that I had is long gone the life that I'm living is not my own, and I want God to use the restored life that He gives for Him alone. I don't to use that life like the conceited life that I had before. In June 9, 2014 I was transferred to a group home. The group home that I was in had the best therapy program. Within one year I was in therapy there I got discharged from all therapy, thank God.

Since I got there the people who lived in the same house with me think that just because I can walk I think that I was better than them which was not true at all. Those people where they seated was not a place for me to be because they don't watched their mouth at all. They talked so dirty that they were always give dirty jokes that's why I never seat between them because the Bible says in / Psalms 1:1-2 Blessed is the man who walks not in the counsel of the wicked, nor stand in the way of sinners, nor sits in the seat of scoffers; but delight is in the law of the Lord, and on his law he meditates day and night".

Therefore, I was always in my rooms it's either watching TBN a Christian channel, or reading my bible. Since then, they thought that I think that I'm better than them just because I can walk. There were one of them that was always cursing at me what I used to do was going into my room cry my eyes out. One day he felt like to curse me I got so mad I was just eating in the dining room I slapped my hand on the table said that enough is enough because I didn't do anything to him, he just decided to curse me and he did. Because I never answered him when he cursed at me, he took advantage of cursing me every time he gets a chance.

That day he called me the devil child because I got so mad at him ever since then he never bothers me again. I finally got peace in the house because every time he cursed at me, I told the house manager on him, and the house manager told me that: you know that he has a brain injury, so the manager came and the man always apologize, and start doing the same thing over and over again.

He even used that I know that he had a brain injury just like the house manager told me. I got so tired that I always bring my pains to the God Almighty because I know that only God can deliver me from that mess. In the Friday morning after Thanksgiving the staff was screaming at me, and I got so upset that I started screaming back at them which was not the solution.

The reason why they were screaming at me was because the girl staff finished showering the woman in the wheelchair, and somewhat the cover of the toilet bowl was dirty, and I wiped it before I sat on it to take off my clothes before I went to the shower room, and I forgot to flush the toilet as I went to dress up myself the girl staff was screaming my name. When you're looking at me right now, and see my accident pictures you will understand what I mean by that verse. In my experience with God; I believe that I was in God University, and I had to go through trials in my life. The Christian life doesn't mean everything will be smooth all the way because Jesus even told that in (John 16:33). That's why I never discouraged because James 1:2-4 says that the trials are not here to kill us, but to test our faith to make us grow stronger in Christ Jesus.

The trials gave me the strength, because every time the trials came to my life, I said to myself "it is all in God's plan. Because I know that God has a plan in my life, and God brought me back to life for a reason. When doctors gave me five percent chance to wake up in the coma that was in for three months, and the doctor called my spiritual mother aside to tell her that I dead, so he just didn't know how to tell my father. I believe that it was all in the plans, and I accept it just like it is. Because I know after trials is glory that's why I do not complain about the situation. In order to know who and what God is and can do "you have to go through all the difficulties there is in His plans." like I said the trials are not there to kill us, but to make us stronger.

I went through a lot of pain in the group home. I was so independent I didn't need anybody to do stuff for except for cooking. I was not allowed to cook because they were afraid that I would've burn their house. One morning I went to shower and before I felt like I had to pee, and I wipe the toilet bowl to seat. I put the tissue in the toilet bowl since I couldn't pee, I forgot to flush the toilet. That was when one of the staff shouted my name. "Come to flush the toilet because I want to use it, but I didn't use the toilet. All I did was wipes the seat, and I forgot to flush the paper it" since I was dressing myself I told her that I was busy because I was dressing myself to go to the place that we had the therapy. She was pressured me, and I flushed the toilet when I was done dressing myself, and as I went to the kitchen she said to me "go flush the toilet" I got so upset, and I screamed back at her.

The man staff was screaming at me said to me "you call yourself a Christian which they always used against me after they start to scream at me. "I couldn't stand to get screamed at, and I started shouting, and crying, and the girl even asked me to mop the floor after I took a shower, and I told her that I was not doing her job for her because I paid her to do her job it was not my job to do. Both of them answered me "you paid us with what money, the state paid us, and I said nothing anymore after they told me so.

I said to myself, it's a part of the plan It's just a test according to James 1:2- 3 Count it all joy, my brothers, when you meet trials of various kinds, verse 3 says that for you know that the testing of your faith produces steadfastness, to go to the 4th verse it's also says that "And let steadfastness have its full effect, that you may be perfect and complete, lacking in nothing. And I always knows that it's just an experience that God is doing with me because all the great servant of God suffers, and I asked God to strengthen me because God never give us more than we can handle.

They treated me as handicap at all times just because of my accident which I didn't like at all. I had had my driving license since 2012 and after I was done, or got discharged with all my therapy I had a trust fund that promised me they would buy a car for me, and pay for the assurance of the car for me since they made me that promise after I was done with therapy I called them to tell them about it in order for them to buy me thee car, and said "no you have to took another driving test again, and I agreed to take it, and they suggest to take it in one the Rehabilitation because they had a program that could help me get back driving.

They said to me that they are going to let me go back to the road without retesting, and I agreed with them therefore took the driving test again. When I passed the driving test I went to look for a car that need. They said that the want a meeting with me, so I went to the meeting. What killing is that the meeting was about the fact I lived in their property I could not own a car, so since they have apartment I asked them for an apartment. They told me that their apartment was not available. I know that if something like that happen is because it wasn't in God's plan for me to get an apartment. God's plan for me is greater than my plan.

The reason why I asked them for the apartment was because I know that they have a lot of people who live in their apartment that own cars.

Since I was finished with therapy mid-2015, and they always bring me to the rehab just to do nothing I was so tired of it. I told them that I want to get a job, and get my own apartment therefore they agreed. You know you get more tired when you're not doing anything just like if you were working eight hours shift on your feet. In facts you can get even more tired from doing nothing.

I had to pee so bad one time, so I run the bell for somebody to come bring me to the bathroom nobody came. And I rung it more than six or seven staff were in the floor since no one came to help. Since no one came to help me, I tried to go by myself, and I felt thank God I wasn't hurt that bad, but I hit my left arm that I have the metal on. It was hurt, and I was crying like a baby. I didn't have the right side of my head the doctor gave me a helmet to wear to protect my head, and it was so far from me because nobody thought that incident was going to happen. I spent the whole night in the hospital. The doctors did several tests for me "Ct Scan, and every order test that they thought would help. Thank Jesus everything was great.

The God of Shadrach, Meshach, and Abednego is still the same. What God did for them He still doing it today, and can do it for you as well like He rose me from death. Remember that He did it before in the New Testament He rose Lazarus after he was buried for four days in a tomb (John 11). Read your bible, and you see what God promised Joshua in "Joshua 1:8 This Book of the Law shall not depart from your mouth, but you shall meditate on it day and night, so that you may be careful to do according to all that is written in it. For then you will make your way prosperous, and then you will have good success."

I asked him "what are my medical condition?" and he told me that your doctor was the one who sent you here right? I just agreed to take the evaluation because the nurse at the group home that I was in asked me kindly, my trust fund director in order for her to pay the car for me agreed to pay it for me. I took six lessons after that they asked to go car shopping, and I went to a first dealer for an Acura they told me that they couldn't pay for a brand-new car for me, and I told them "No problem." I'm going to explain why did I have a trust fund. My dad took a lawyer to plead the accident for me, and he came to meet me at the group home to have me sign the papers for that to happen.

He got me to sign it before my dad came. The lawyer told me that I couldn't have any money in my name because the hospital was going to take all the money that I had in my name because I didn't have Medicare then. So that money needs to put in a trust for me, and I agreed to sign the papers. After the meeting with the lawyer the trust director came to tell me how the trust work.

She told me that the money they hold for me how I can spend it. The thing was that she explained clearly to me that she will send me a credit card here is how I could use it. I could not buy anything to eat with it not even a candy. If I need a car even pay for the car insurance for me, cloths, even wedding dress they can buy all this for me. The feeding me part was no a very big deal because God took great of me. God always provides for me to eat.

They can pay a hotel room for me if go to vacation, and also pay the plan ticket for me. When I went to Haiti in August, they paid for the plan ticket for me. Having a trust fund was not so bad after all. They pay all my bills and everything wisely I use to think of them as an unfair business, but they're not so unfair after all rules are rules. That was very fair, but I didn't think of it fairly until now. My bills are paid on time, and I'm happy. The only thing I was tired of was to imprisoned at the group home. Imagine I wake up every morning to get ready to go in the rehab where I used to have therapy every 8:30 to 3:30 doing nothing there just because the house manager didn't want to leave me in house by myself, and I had no choice to go with the other patients, and do nothing there just to play games: such as Connect four, and any other games that could my brain to improve. when I could've used that time in a classroom to learn. I don't like playing games because games are for babies not for me a 29 years old woman. Even when I was a baby, I didn't like to play game, and now as 29 years old I found myself playing games. This was a humiliation right there. I sign up for online University, and didn't like online school at all. I wanted to get out of the group home to get out of all these childish activities. I understood, it was for brain, but I beat all the staffs in every game that they thought me. Like I said God has a perfect time for everything. When the time came, I got out. Thank God.

Some people didn't understand that, I was capable of being independent. I could cook, all I needed was someone to clean my place for me. I think it was all about the money. They could think of many excuses to tell me, so they could keep me there, but I couldn't take it no more. They're willing to pay another driving test for me, but not the and I like the car the I got. The reason why I believed that they were paying for the car for me was because I went on vacation to Haiti on August, they paid for the plane ticket for me. I could say that they got me fooled really, but I am done on being fooled "no more fooling around" I am really done with this fooling around because I don't like the way I've been treated by everyone who thinks that I'm stupid just because I was a TBI patient.

He could not clear me from driving, and each lesson I had to bring more money at every time I was supposed to come for the driving test. Since the greedy money man didn't want to clear me of driving although he wasn't teaching me how to drive; he gave me all mistakes that was from the book of mistakes just to get more money. He kept telling me how an excellent driver that I was, but couldn't clear me from driving. One of the days he crushed my spirit by telling me "Only if I have 15 more lesson with him. I told him "Don't even think about it." I took my strength to tell him so and my case manager at the group home asked me to give him her number, and her Ext, so I did.

After the last test I told him about it, but he told me no he couldn't call her therefore he didn't take her number from me. I went to tell her what he told me about calling her. She called him right before me, and he didn't answer the phone. I didn't know that they had a driving school at Kessler where I was in for rehabilitation "I realized they have the driving school when I went back to visit the rehabilitation for the first time after two years, and saw they have a student driver school over there as well I said to myself why didn't I came back after my last surgery? Because I knew if I stayed over there, I was going to have my driving test again without charging all that money.

She left a message for him, and that's when he reported to her that I need multiple tasks, and she agreed with what he told her. So, she encouraged me to take the test again, and I agreed "but I don't want the same instructor again because that man is full of himself that I couldn't deal with his sneaky self. What he believed since she has a brain injury why not take advantage of her, so he told me that my doctor was the one that send me there they since I didn't know who my doctor was because ever since my last surgery, I never see my doctor again.

He gave me six test, and he always says the same thing. The second time I went for the test before he gave me the test he asked me, do you bring the $198? and I asked what is it for? he told that's the rules and he gave me the check that I already paid $394 already, he thought that just because I had the brain injury, so I was crazy. He was almost not giving the test that day, and he went outside telling me that he went to talk to his boss as he went outside I started praying, and he came back to tell me that he changed his mind he will give me the test as he was finished testing me he said the same thing over, and over again "you are an excellent driver, but I can't clear you because of your medical condition.

It's all about the money with that man. Even at my last lesson with him, through all the drive, he didn't say anything until I was done, and parked the car. He asked me what do you think? And I said to him that he is the instructor just tell me, and he said to me I know you were looking forward for me to clear you from driving, but I can't because your medical condition can just pop up just like that. I don't know what was his deal because he was teaching me how to drive, I had my driver's license since 2010 "yeah I get it know he wanted more money. He didn't have to do all this to get more money out of me all he has to do is to simply asked me for the money.

Just because I got hit by a car doesn't make me dumb for that. Thanks to the Lord God Jesus Christ I have a better memory, and understanding. What he didn't know that I was a smart girl for somebody who had a brain injury.

Do I sound like a nonsense person to you guys that reading my book? A lot of people think that just because I was injured in my head it was impossible for me to remember stuff. The right skull of my head spent 5 months out in laboratory to China. Like the Spirit of God talked to my heart to let me know to do not trouble myself because I have the promise of God in my life. Remember what Isaiah 41:10 says. God was the one that was spoken to His people:

Fear not, for I am with you; be not dismayed, for I am your God; I will strengthen you, I will help you, I will uphold you with my righteous right hand. I love that song: Because He live, I can face tomorrow" I kept saying just like the bible tells us God never start something without finishing it as Apostle Paul says in Philippians 1:6 And I am sure of this, that He who began a good work in you will bring it to completion at the day of Jesus Christ.

By that I mean that the same God who rose me from the death will complete the works that He started in my life. He restored my soul like David says in Psalms 23;1-3 The Lord is my shepherd; I shall not want.2 He makes me lie down in a green pasture.3 He restored my soul. He leads me in paths of righteousness for His name's sake. You know the rest of the verse. I also believe in Jeremiah 29;11 For I know the plans I have for you, declares the Lord, plans for welfare and not for evil, to give a future and hope. I believe in that plan because God didn't let me die for a reason.

The plan God has over my life as to accomplish. I also believe in what Psalmist David says in Psalms 118:12-18. 12 They surrounded me like bees; they went out like a fire among thorns; in the name of Lord, I cut them off! 13. I was pushed hard, so that I was falling, but the Lord helped me. 14 The Lord is my strength and my song; He has become my salvation. 15 Glad songs of salvation are in the tents of the righteous; The right hand of the Lord does valiantly, 16 the right hand of the Lord exalts, the right hand of the Lord does valiantly! 17 I shall not die, but I shall live, and recount the deeds of the Lord.

The Lord has disciplined me severely, but He has not given me over to death. The Lord loves me, so I don't to ask God why things happened to me because Romans 8:28 says that "And we know that for those who love God all things work together for good, for those who are called according to His purpose. I love the words of God so much every promise that's in the words of God for our purpose in life. Some time we are going to a difficulty in our life when we open the Bible you might surprise to see as you open the Bible, and you end up to a passage that talked about what you are going through. You might think "oh what a coincidence? but it not it is not a coincidence because God know what you're going through.

Remember that Jesus came in flesh, He went through worse, just to know our pain. Before you ask God "why me? think about Jesus at the cross who was punished for our sins a sin that He did not commit. The father could not even look at him because God is a Holy God that see the sins upon His son just for sake Jesus went through all this. God is a good God. Think about the love God has for humanity.

This afternoon I took a nap as I woke up and I was sharing my testimony with some people that doesn't even know me, and one of them told me as I was sharing my accident pictures with them she told that Jesus loves you so much and I said yes He does, and I love Him because I would be in the grave for two years now if it wasn't for His love. God bless you all for reading that testimony, and remember that God love you unconditionally. It doesn't matter who you are, or what you have done. He still loves you. God bless you all.

It's not a story; it's a reality what I'm talking about it's not just a story God really did all these things in my life. He can also do it for you as well, as long as you believe in Him, and knows that He is a powerful God that was from the ancient day. His nature never changed. He is Alpha and Omega, the Beginning and the End if you read the book of Revelation, you will see what I meant by that because it's in the book of Revelation. I believe that it's just a beginning "I mean more testimony coming in my life, and I never going to give up because I've come too far the way I started from. God brought me too far to live me." Remain bless with Christ Jesus.

THE DAYS IN THE HOSPITAL

DIAGNOSES: (1) Subarachnoid hemorrhage. (2) Epidural hemorrhage. (3) Multiple basilar skull fractures. (4) Fractured left humerus. (5) Respiratory failure. (6) Hypokalemia. (7) Hypoxia. (8) Hyperglycemia. (9) Acute blood loss anemia. (10) Malnutrition. (11) Multi- bacterial pneumonia. (12) Respiratory insufficiency. (13) Clostridium difficile infection. (14) Left 12th rib fracture. (15) The left temporoparietal skull fracture.

PROCEDURES: Base on my medical record I found out how and what my medical procedure where like. (1) On 08/27/2013, I underwent craniotomy, craniectomy, and a subdural hematoma with JP drains left in subgalea the doctor from Neurosurgery. (2) On 08/27/2013, I again underwent a craniotomy. I had a left temporal lobectomy and evacuation of epidural hematoma. The second craniotomy was by a Neurosurgeon doctor who treated me at the time. (3) On 08/28/2013, I underwent a central line placement, triple-lumen catheter by one of the doctors. (4) On 08/30/2013, I underwent a bedside trach and PEG by a doctor. (5) On 08/30/2013, also I underwent a bronchoscopy with BAL by the same doctor. (6) On 09/04/2013, I again underwent a bronchoscopy and BAL by another doctor. (7) On 09/03/2013, I underwent an open reduction and internal fixation of my left humerus by the doctor of the Orthopedic Department.

HISTORY OF MY ILLNESS AND HOSPITAL COURSE:

At 27 -years -old; I was a pedestrian struck with a positive **LOC**. I was struck at a unknown rate of speed. I was found by **EMS** unresponsive, apparently posturing on scene. I was intubated in the field by **ALS**, and according to **ALS**, I was thrown approximately 150 feet per bystander. On arrival, I had a **GCS** of 40. I had a heart rate of 110 to 120. My blood pressure was 127/88. I was saturating initially at 100% bag valve mask, went up to 99% with institution of increased bagging. My right pupil was fixed dilated. The left pupil was approximately 4 mm and minimally reactive. I had a noticed left temporoparietal scalp laceration, which protruded down past the skull.

I was endotracheally intubated orally. My breath sound was coarse bilaterally. I had no crepitus. Heart sounds were normal. My abdomen was soft and nondistended. Pelvis was stable. I did have positive radial and ulnar pulses bilaterally with a gross deformity to the left humerus. I had abrasions to the left hip region. On arrival to the trauma Bay as well, I was log rolled. The back was palpated. No step-offs were palpated. I had chest x-ray done, which showed that the endotracheal tube was in good position. I had an OGT placed, which returned thick dark blood with food.

Temp- sensing Foley catheter was placed, which had clear yellow urine returned. I had an **ABE** done in Trauma Bay, which revealed a base deficit of -11 and a lactate of 8.6. I had some haziness on the chest x-ray, although no noted pneumothorax. I underwent a **FAST** examination, which was reportedly negative by the doctor in the Emergency Department. I was hemodynamically stable and was brought to the **CAT** scan. In the **CAT** scan, there was noted right parietal subdural hematoma with a significant midline shift as well as diffuse cerebral edema. There was a left temporoparietal skull fracture as well as basilar skull fracture noted.

The **CAT** scan of my neck was negative for any fractures, and my chest revealed bilateral pulmonary contusions and a left 12th rib fracture as well and haziness in the lungs. The **CT** of abdomen pelvis revealed no intra-abdominal injuries. While in the **CAT** scan, we initiated 1 gram of Cerebyx, and also through her second **IV** line, we initiated 100 grams of mannitol. The patient had received a Tdap Boostrix vaccination. She was also medicated with fentanyl for possible pain. I was sedated with small amount of Propofol. On completion of the **CAT** scan, the patient was emergently taken to the operating room by the doctor of the Neurosurgery Department for a craniectomy, craniotomy, and evacuation of clot.

Post OR procedure, the patient was admitted to the Surgical Intensive Care Unit, where I was monitored. I was hemodynamically stable, although they noted protrusion of the area where the skull as removed. I was emergently taken back to the Operating Room after having a repeat **CAT** scan of the head. I underwent the second craniotomy, craniectomy, and had evacuation of the epidural hematoma with a temporal lobectomy. At that time, she had a central line placed in the Operating Room as well by the Anesthesia Team. On completion of the second OR procedure, the patient went down for an additional repeat **CAT** scan of the head, which showed some infarcts. I also had some pneumocephalus noted on the repeat **CAT** scan after the second craniectomy.

I was being monitored in the Surgical Intensive Care Unit, remains intubated with a tidal volume of 500, rate of 12, **PEEP** of 8, and 75% O2, **CMV** mode. I have remained sedated and will be continued on antiepileptic therapy. I also had labs drawn from the Trauma Admitting Area for routine labs, **CBC, BMP,** type and crossed for 6. Point of care pregnancy test was negative. While in Surgical Intensive Care Unit, I will be initiated on enteral feeding secondary to the fact that she will be unable to sustain nutrition. I spiked the temp to 101.4. My heart rate remained in 100s with a blood pressure of 100/64 to 121/68, heart rate anywhere from 95 to 134s.

I was started also on 08/28/2013 on hypertonic saline and will be started on Fiber source enteral feedings 250 mL q.4 h. I was also placed on a cooling blanket and had some issues with hyperglycemia, so an insulin drip was initiated also to keep her euglycemic, especially giving the fact that she is being started on enteral feeds. Hyperglycemia was probably secondary to the brain injury since there was no history given as per the parents, who responded to the hospital that patient had no past medical history, surgical history, no meds, and denied any allergies to any medications. On 08/30/2013, patient's hemoglobin down to 6.9.

The patient was given the facts 2 units of packed red blood cells, which increased her post transfusion hemoglobin to 8. She does have on 08/30/2013 positive corneal, gag, and cough. **GCS** was 70 at the time. I continued to spike fever as 09/01/2013. I was empirically started on vancomycin and Zosyn on 08/30/2013, which she continues to spike up 102.4. The rest of her vital signs remained stable. Blood pressure approximately 100 to the 110s heart rate anywhere from mid 90s to the 130s. On 09/01/2013, I did have a bilateral infiltrate on the chest x-ray. **DVT** prophylaxis was initiated at that time. On 09/02/2013, the vancomycin was discontinued and 09/05/2013, I was started on p.o. Vancomycin.

I remain in the (**SICU**) is the Intensive Care Unit spiking fevers and tachycardia. I remained with enteral tube- feedings, now via my **PEG**. I remained on the ventilator, although I was breathing spontaneously over the vent. On 09/10/2013, they initiated trach collar trials for this patient and weaned me off the sedation. I was then being followed by the PM&R specialist doctor as well for **TBI**. On 09/10/13, also I started to open my eyes spontaneously, although I was not following commands at this time. On 09/12/2013, I was cleared for transfer out to a **PCU** setting.

I was on trach collar, which I was successfully weaned off the ventilator. I had been transfused 3 times now. On 09/03/2013, in the **OR**, I had 2 units of packed red blood cells for hemoglobin that dropped down to 6.9 with **EBL** on that procedure for the ORIF of approximately 700 mL of blood. I also received 2 bottles of albumin. On 09/13/2013, I was transferred to **PCU**. On 09/16/2013, my trach was downsized to #6. I was opening my eyes spontaneously. At times, I did trach, but I was still not following commands. My sutures were removed from my scalp prior to this entry. Prior to approximately 09/12/2013, they were removed. The doctor also ordered helmet for me, so that I could be out of bed, into structure chair. PT/OT has been working with me throughout.

With range of motion, I had a hand splint on to the right and a sling is maintained to the left for the humerus fracture. I remained hemodynamically stable, has completed courses of antibiotics for my multi-bacterial pneumonia as well as my C. diff. p.o vancomycin and Flagyl that since has subsided and had been removed from isolation. My JP drained were removed on 08/30/2013 by Neurosurgery. Was being set up for rehab Facility at Kessler. My family were involved the entire time with picking out institution. I was accepted to Kessler Rehab Institute in Saddle Brook on 09/20/2013. My family was in much agreement.

I was localizing mildly and I was more awake and alert on 09/20/2013, although I was not verbal, nor did I grossly follow commands. I remained with a foley to bedside drainage, which would be removed at Kessler Institute. I would be continued to be followed by the PM&R staff at Kessler Institute for my TBI (Traumatic Brain Injury). I was discharged in stable condition with follow up with the previous doctor in the Doctor's Office Center as needed. I also had followed up for Neurosurgery and my ultimate skull replacement with Dr. X upon discharge from Kessler.

Cried for the guidance
of The Holy Spirit

On January 1st, 2016, I thank God for adding one years to my life, and allow me to see the year of 2016. My new year resolutions are to get closer to God, and for God Will to be done in my life. I give myself a way to God; and for God to use as a tools in His Kingdom. I believe that God will deliver me from myself because I did not want to live my life just the way I wanted anymore. For, I am now a new creation in Jesus. I decided to let 2 Corinthians 5: 17 to be activated in my life.

I pray that for God to change me completely as the new year changed. I don't want to live my life the same way I lived it in 2015. I'm the light in this World, and I want my light to shine everywhere I go because I don't like the way I was in 2015. I dedicate myself to God to do what He please with me, and I knew I had bad habits such as "I don't like to be bother by anybody; I could get very angry at people who keep on running their mouth without knowing a story, and they enter to the scene without any invitations.

I would love for God to renew my memories as well because I don't know what happened. When I started writing that book God used to give me what to write in it while I taking a nap when I woke up in the morning, I remember everything, so I put them in it even if I don't write it right away when I woke up. As I got to the program where I used to have therapy, I always remembered everything even put more in it.

I do not understand what's happening now when God revealed me something at night the next morning, I can't even remember what God revealed me to put in it. God, please renew my memory to remember everything that you reveal me to put in it, or wake me up to start writing everything. That's why I started written the chapter three because God revealed to me what to write in it. Since God approved of me to write that book, I believe that He will always reveal what He want me to put in it even in my sleep.

I had the most wonderful time at the House of Prayer's Annual Thanksgiving. I really miss those days back in the day; I never miss a day at the services, but now I have no choice because they put me in a group home meaning I'm not independent like I used to be anymore. I know that chain will break for me in this new year of 2016. Nothing is impossible for God to do. God came from too far with me to leave me. I believe that God has a better plan for my life because He did not give me over death on the 27th of August 2013. I receive and I claim all the blessing that God have over my life in the name of Christ Jesus.

I was so excited to be back in House of Prayer one more time, and I don't think it's just a temporary. I love House of Prayer member especially my Spiritual mother; who gave me that assignment to start written a book about the Testimony Of my life because God gives me a life testimony; I was going through something that I didn't understand where does it came from, so I called her to explain to her what was going on. She gave me that advice to keep myself busy, and I listened to her advice and I started written ever since then I found the solutions to what I was going through.

When I go to House of Prayer everybody treats me like a princess, and I love the way that they treat me. Praise God; when I was at the rehab you would never believe it how they treated me. That's why I felt like God gives me a family that I never had before. Not even from my biological family I never feel that kind of love that I receive from my Spiritual family that God gives me. My biological family thought I didn't want to work because I was a lazy girl, but they didn't know the plan of God for my life. I talked about that in chapter One in my book it's just a way to express my love for my Spiritual family. I love God so much I can't wait to see me coming back to work for God because I really miss it.

On the beginning of April, 2016, I felt a way that I never felt before like a pregnant lady in contraction. First, I felt bloated, then my stomach was hurting me. I even took med for it because I didn't understand what was happening to me. On that Sunday, 2016 I felt even worst, but I was invited to testify at one of the churches that was praying for me to give my testimony. The Church name is Prophecy Church of God. When I got there the pain came, and I tried to see if I can use the restroom still nothing.

Before I left the church, I prayed in my heart for God to reveal the pastor to pray with me because something didn't feel right. As I went to the restroom again in my way back from the bathroom my ride came to tell me that the bishop wants to prayed for me before I left. I praise God for answering my prayers very fast. They prayed with me and it was like I was giving birth to a baby that's how hard was the pain that I had.

As I arrived to my aunt's house I started vomiting, and as I was vomiting, I pushed so hard and I accidently go on myself. I know it's an embarrassing story, but I have to write it in my book because it a part of my testimony. When I knocked in my aunt door no one was there I vomited even more so my ride gave me some water to drink, and I stop vomiting at the time. My ride saw the way I was calling for Jesus to help me, so he waited for me he dropped me at my friend's house.

That's why I told you guys that the true family is in God. As I arrived at my friend's house, I was screaming on Jesus to deliver me from the pain. Everybody was asking me if I was ok; I couldn't even talk and I went straight to the bathroom. I spent an hour and a half in the toilet bowl. After I got out of the bathroom I felt like to go straight to bed; I breath so heavy then my friend's mother saw the pain I was in, and she asked one of her children to bring me to my house.

I told her that I was supposed to be in church at this time; she said "you cannot go to church the way I see you, "so she sent somebody to drove me home. When I got home; I changed my cloths and go back to the bathroom. Even though I couldn't go so I tried. It was so hard for me to go I took my evening meds so I went to bed.

As I laid in the bed my stomach was growling with gas; I cried on Jesus to help me, so Jesus delivered me from all the pains. You see the

Mighty God that we serve. Including Him in all little things in our lives; He will intervene and deliver us from anything that we're going through. Just trust in Him because nothing is impossible for Him to do.

In Friday the 15/fifteen of 2016 I felt a depression that I never felt before. I went to bible sturdy in my church; I was very well when I got there, and all the sudden I felt so depressed after a while. As I came from the church my ride dropped me to my house; I felt worse. I went to prayer, and I ask God to strengthen me after the prayer I went straight to bed. I slept, but in Saturday morning I woke up with tears in my eyes. So, I asked my brothers and sisters in to keep me in their prayers.

Some of them told me "do not be discouraged; read your bible. In the morning before I even brush my teeth the first thing I do is to send the Bible verse to all my contacts, and I told them that I already read my Bible. Tears could not stop from my eyes, and I said to myself it is the words of God "what arm would It does to me? before I opened my Creole my Bible I prayed to the Holy Spirit to help find a passage according to what I was going through.

And I opened my Creole Bible exactly in John 16 that talk about "The work of the Holy Spirit, and The Disciples' Grief Will Turn to joy." Praise God it was exactly what I wanted. I love the parable that Jesus was telling the Disciples in the 20th -22th verses. When they didn't understand Jesus's parable, and they started to speak among each other; Jesus Told them in the verse of 20th; Very truly I tell you, you will weep and mourn while the world rejoices. You will grieve, but your grief will turn to joy.

In the 21 verse Jesus said something very strong to them. I love this A woman giving birth to a child has pain because of her time has come; but when her baby is born into, she forgets the anguish because of her joy that a child is born into the world. The 22nd verse Jesus told them; So, with you: Now is your time of grief, but I will see you again and you will rejoice, and no one will take away your joy. Thank You Lord for Your promise Words in the Bible that gives me strength to deal with my trials.

Thank you, Lord. After reading the scriptures God strength came back to me. I was so happy that the Holy Spirit brought me straight to those scriptures. I was feeling with joy that Jesus was telling the Disciples about. Through out of the day, I received a call from one of the brethren's that I have fellowship with. He told me that God put in his heart to call me, and he prayed for deliverance with me.

In the same April, 2016 I received a special call from a special woman of God from my church, the woman president leader: I appreciated the call so much we talked for an hour and half. She was telling me a revelation that God gave her for me and I explained to her what I was going through in my life that was a confirmation about the dream that God gave her about me. She prayed with me in the phone. The prayer was more about deliverance, and healing.

She also spoke blessing about my life. It was so wonderful to know how much God was thinking, care about me. I love God; He never leave me nor forsake me. He always sends somebody to pray with me when I'm going through tough time in my life. I don't even have to explain anything to anybody, and God already tell them about my situations. Isn't God awesome?

How I thought that I was in a relationship with somebody, and I realized that I was the only one in the relationship. How I felt so stupid about the facts because it really was embarrassing. I always tell that story to every guy who think that they are interested in me. I don't know when I will stop telling that story, but I am praying for it to be over soon. I said that I didn't need anybody in my life just because of that bad first experience. I thought that all men are the same: it was a hard time of my life that I never wanted to deal with any man ever in my life.

I was so curious about it until I spoke to the woman of God. This is not the plan of God for my life: God has something more wonderful and better for me. I believe in Jeremiah 29:11 the plan that God have of my life is the plans of hope not to arm me. All things happen for good to those who love Christ Jesus. If someone was in your life, and leave that because it wasn't meant to be. Just think about it in a positive way.

Don't blame the situation to the other person. It maybe your own fault. A lots of time things like that happens we always blame the other person, so don't do that. God has a second touch of our lives we never really think about instead we blame somebody for our own mistake.

Sometimes we think that we are smarter than God: it's a big mistake my fellow people. Have patient and wait on God.

God loves us so much that in Isaiah 54:16-17 God Himself says "See, it is I who created the blacksmith who fans the coals into flame and forges a weapon fit for its work. And it is I who have created the destroyer to wreak havoc; No weapon forged against you will prevail, and you will refute every tongue that accuses you. This is the heritage of the servants of the Lord, and this is their vindication from me," declares the Lord.

I just now realized something about what I so-called relationship. I really feel ashamed about all the facts on that story. It turned out that, it was never a relationship because I was too stupid to accept the facts base on how close we used to be. Only he was always tell me that he loved me, but it wasn't enough because loving somebody is not what's coming out of your mouth; love is action. Kissing with somebody doesn't really mean that the person really loves you. To go farther even having sex with that person doesn't really mean that he, or she loves. I now learned that base on my experience. I feel so stupid because of those facts.

The thing is I didn't know what love was since I never gave anyone chances, and I didn't know when people are boyfriend and girlfriend. I thought that what I had with him was how a relationship was supposed to be because he asked me to be his girlfriend when I Said "yes "he was already in a big confusion. He was always telling me that he was confused, but I didn't understand his confusion until it was too late.

When that happened to me all I did every day and second was crying because I didn't know how to deal with the facts. By any means, I want you to know that you should always have someone that could talk to. God is waiting to listen to our everyday life story. I was lack of knowledge and everything; first the Words of God, and then this. I'm very embarrassed for written this, but I have no choice, but to tell the truth on how stupid I was just to let that happened to me. I put myself into this mess because I let my mind play trick play trick on me. I felt so comfortable with this guy, and thought that God had sent him as my husband to be. At the end of the story, I got deceived. Young people, let God guide you, and not let you heart deceive you.

To tell you the truth I really did love him a lot unfortunately he was not the one. He took advantage of the facts because I didn't know how these things work. Those who have parents talks to them about your relationship with anybody. Better yet, you have a Father in Heaven who wants you to come to Him with everything in your life. I don't blame him because he is a man; and for what I heard men do that most of the time especially when they don't want you. The thing is he knew what a relationship is since he had several of them before, and knew exactly what he was doing. I always talked like a someone who knew everything wig a big mouth, I was not a woman that can never be a wife for him, and I agreed with him. It is now I understand when he told me once "I was the one that sent him where he is."

That's why he told people that he was never with me because nobody knew about us. When I asked him to tell our parents about it because we went too far already and not a soul knew about us; he asked me to give a little more time, and I agreed with him because he never gave me any sign that he was doing anything like that to me. He just didn't know how to tell me about his relationship with his ex-girlfriend yet, and I even told him how to tell her that he had a girlfriend already because she was always texted him when I was with him.

Cleaver that he was; he always gave me the text to read where asked him if he was the man for her, and I believed him that he had nothing secretive for me (to hide for me) but he had. The way that I taught him to break it to her was the same way that he used to break it to me. At least he learned honesty from me, and I appreciated that. I still felt that I was played by him; the only man that I trusted betrayed me poorly.

That's why I mentioned that I was played by my best friend. Thanks to him I don't have any earthly friends anymore. Don't be surprised to see me said that my only friend and best friend now is Jesus. Christ Jesus is the only person that I trust; because He will never lie to me. Like I said someone can pull a gun trigger to my head please do not lie to me.

What I meant to say is that it was not his fault; it was all my fault because I wasn't supposed to put myself in this situation. Some time I wish that I had never met him; the thing is I didn't understand what was going on in my life at all. Because I rejected so many men who seems to really loved me, and felt for that person that didn't even care about me. After all this happened, I even wish that I never came to New Jersey to meet him at all. Among all the youth choir, there was a lot of young man in the choir, and I had falling for the wrong person. I regret the fact I didn't asked God another confirmation when God told me he was the man of my life. What I understand as a Christian this was in the plan of God. It was a part of the trials of my life. No one to blame but myself because I should've known better.

Things like that happens to girls like me with no experiences. And I'm tired of feeling sorry for myself, so now I'm trying to understand what happened to me doesn't only happen to me. They are so many unfortunate girls out there just like I was who are going through the same things. My advice for them is to do not be discouraged because God has a better plan for each and everyone's life just trust God.

This experience could've ended my life because I never plan on being in relationship with multi men like a woman changes her underwear; I arrived in a point where I said that I never want anything to do with "what you call relationship ever again may the will of God be done in my life. "The reason why I thought that way was because I was hurt so bad; I'm not saying that I wanted to die because in my mind he was the only one for me.

That was how I thought but it was not what God says; sometimes our plans are ahead of God plans which is not a good way to think of things. Let God take control of your lives that's the only way for you to get to the destinations that God has over your lives. Believe me when I say that God has a perfect plan for our lives. Let God works on your lives; you can see that only happen to us girls because we are the weak gender. Be courageous and you will see how God is working mightily in your lives.

As a woman I believe that God is going to do a great miracle in my life, so should you believe as well my sisters. Life is not over. Mankind can say that your life is over, but God has the final say to each one of your lives. It is not over until God says that it is over. We are stronger than that. God time is the best time. Sometimes we made poor choices in our lives because when we were making that choice, we didn't include God to it in advance, and we suffer so much after it.

I'm talking base on my experience; you know when I included God in it. It was when I got into the deep mess, and it was already too late for me. If I invited God first; I would've know it was a trap because God would've tell me clearly. It's not like God didn't tell me that something was going on, but I didn't understand at the time. God showed me in a dream what was going on, but I didn't understand dreams at the time, so as I woke up from the dream I called him to explain what I saw. Only if I believed and understand that the dream I had come from God I would never be in the mess that I was in.

My sisters sometimes God speak to us; He doesn't want you to go around to explain to anyone what He shows you. In going to tell everyone about what God shows us sometimes God changes the plan that He has for us. Stop running your mouth about what God tells us because we can miss out a lot. Even though you may not understand what you see; just go in prayers to ask God about what you see if it's coming from Him or not.

We talk too much; I may say that I talked to much "please forgive me God" it doesn't matter who that person is in your lives when God shows us something do not even tell our spouse about it. Even if our spouse sees us speaking in our sleep, and wakes up beside us do not tell him about your dream because it is something personal between you and God. Our spouse may know it after it comes to pass. I'm not even married yet, but I was listening to a sermon that Evangelist Jean Jacques Taylor preach about that. He made perfect sense about the point.

We talk too much ladies, and it's a big mistake when we talk like that. When we talk like that it doesn't help us at all give our mouth something else to do instead of talking about every detail that we see. As I tell you guys that I wish that I never came to Jersey and meet that young man, but there are somethings in our lives unfortunately that we can never change. Like I mentioned in my previous chapters if I had the power to change my pass; I would change the fact that I ever knew that man.

I'm not bitter, nor crazy; I'm just a heartbroken soul, and written this is the only way I could express myself after all these years. I know that you may not understand my pains which I don't ask you to put yourself in my shoes because you would never understand me. I'm just giving the young ladies, advice about the choice that they're making to always put God first to all of your choices that they're making in order for them not to end up a heart broken like me.

What I love about God when I was going through all this, He put people toward me to tell me that He knows what I was going through, and He was always with me. He always shows me that He was with me all the way that's how awesome God is. Even when we don't know He always looking after us. I know what I'm telling you because I've been through it therefore, I know what I'm talking about base on my experience with God.

As you see I made a promise never to go back writing in the chapter two of my book anymore because just thinking about the experience was too painful for me. Since I'm not the one to put anything that I wanted in book therefore I had no choice but to write what the Holy Spirit put in my heart in it. That's why I end up continuing the second chapter in the third chapters. Whatever I write in my book is not coming from me; it's like I have a replay button in my heart that tells me when or what to write.

I was hoping that chapter three had nothing to do with chapter two, but for some reason things from chapter two keep on coming in my mind. I also have a feeling that something will definitely happen after all. Remember the book call "The Testimony of My Life "when added everything together it makes complete sense that's what I believe. I have victory over all that is the way I think of it.

I also have something to share with those when they see me, and mention to me that I look already look like a married woman; I didn't know that women who are married has a look. And also tell me that I needed a boyfriend. Please stop telling what I want, we're always thank about what we want, but in question is what we need. Only God knows what we need. The truth is, I don't appreciate that at all. I don't know what you guys were expected from me if you thought that I would've been a wrinkle grandma, so please stop telling me that you're going to look for a boyfriend for me.

I'm not desperate to have a boyfriend, and if God wants me to have someone in my life I believe that He will send him to me. So stop acting like you are Jesus or something because I only trust that Jesus for He has been preparing a prince for me somewhere, and I'm waiting on the Lord with all my heart and believe that He also knows my existence (remember the Haitian proverb that says "Cat burned from a hot water and when it sees cold water and flees away from it; that's me.)I do not asked anyone for boyfriend please telling me that you're going to get one for me please stop because I do not appreciated at all, and I am not desperate for a man." Yes, I know that I am a beautiful lady, but just because I am beautiful doesn't mean that I'm supposed to have a boyfriend.

Some people that are prettier than me and more beautiful than me inside in out, and God did not call them to be married just to serve God the way that He wants them to, and that's why I was praying for God to take all my flesh desires away from me until He send me the prince that He has for me. Meaning if God created me to be a single servant of His I have no choice to be like God created me to be, and may His will be done to my life. I also believe that marriage is not for everyone.

And Apostle Paul says in 1 Corinthians 7:8-9 (Now to the unmarried and the widows I say: It is good for them to stay unmarried, as I do.9 But if they cannot control themselves, they better to marry than to burn with passion.) I'm not going to do something just because my friends are doing it, because God knows my strength, and how my flesh operate. I'm not going to force myself into marriage if it's not in the will of because I see what marriage today are going through because God never approve of their marriages, and I don't want to be one like them.

God knows who is going to be a good husband for me, and when God arranged something for somebody He always give His children good things because He knows us all. So please stop it because I don't ask anybody for anything. Leave me alone please because God is on my case. It is not for you to decide when I need somebody in my life because my life is in God's hand, and He knows exactly when He will send my prince to me.

Thank you so much I just need anyone that wanted to play that role in my life even if it was one of my family I hate the facts (you do realized, and see that I didn't say that I don't like it, but I use the "H" word which is stronger than I do not like it, or I don't appreciated)so please understand me for using that word. It is very offensive to me when you do that. Like yesterday was an international Holiday calling "Valentine's Day" my friends was saying to me happy Valentine's Day. I replied to them that only one day is not going to be enough for me to celebrate "Love Day for me.

When I get married every day will be love day for me and my husband because love is not one day celebration; it is an action the way you treat your spouse or your family. I'm a very romantic woman, so love will be every day thing in my house. I always believe in true love ever since I was a little bit younger because I used to watch a lot of movies about love when I used to live in Haiti and the way the movies end "they were always love at the end of them, and it was always my dream to have true love in my life because love is to beautiful.

The Bible tells us what true love is. God so love the World that He committed an action by giving His only Son to die for humanity. I was so found in love songs. I was always singing love songs even though I never had a boyfriend when I was in Haiti. French love songs was my life before I know the true meaning of being a born again Christian, but now they don't interest me anymore, but I still believe in true love. It's exist because God Himself is love. As a woman I will never go looking for love, but love will find me wherever I am.

I used to watch "shows or Feuilleton about love so much; they told me it was just a scene, or in French they call it montage, but to me it was true love. Once I thought that I found my true love, but unfortunately it was based on lies. That make me realized something at the experience that I had years ago; it is not saying the word that tell you the person love you for real. Players are very good at saying the word, and to make you believe that you are very special to them if you felt for their trick like I did you will end up with a broken hearted like I did. Be smart about that kind of things people. I talked like that because I've been through the situation before and I know what I'm talking about.

Players are not written in the person's face. The nice looking fellow that you see every day that's telling you that he loves you can be the player. At first he can be very nice telling you how much he cares for you; and you are one of the kind; and that you are amazing just way you are. I'm telling you when that song came out he thought that this was the words I wanted to hear, but he was wrong. He used to pass that song for me every time that we met. For some reason they were always pass that song to every radio station especially when we were together. That's the reason why I hate that song now because I don't believe in words that's coming out of anybody mouth.

Imagine after telling me all these words, and he was telling his friends and family that I was not a nice person; I had a lots of attitude. Maybe I had the attitude because he was lying to me, and I didn't have a role model in my family to teach me what I should've known about relationship. All the lovey dove things that he used to tell me was all a lied just because he thought that what I wanted to hear which was false I don't want to hear anything from anybody if it's not the truth.

Please be smart my sisters to know when someone's trying to fool you just to get something from you and the thing that they want from you is something very special to you. It is to discover your promise land. As soon that he discovers it "you mean nothing to him anymore, and he never knows you. Before he used to treat you with respect and then after using you and get what they want. You meant nothing to him just like a pile of garbage.

Everybody said that ladies are a weak sex of all, but with Jesus we are strong. Even I, was fooled by a man that I used to call my best friend. That was one of my weaknesses, and it will never happen again because I have learned from my mistake. Before I never let anybody come near me, but because I wanted to know what it feels like to have someone in my life "I felt in a big mess.

There is something that defined the Will of God of anyone's life. First there is 'the permissive Will of God and the perfect Will of God. The difference between those two are very simple. The permissive Will of God is very dangerous. Sometimes we see something and we want it what we do as a Christian "we prayed about God in His Omnipotent knows that it is not the best thing for you, and don't say anything regarding it. Therefore, we insist about it at the end we end up making the poorest choice in our lives even when God reveal it to a servant, and the servant we believe what we want to believe and do what we want anyway. It's the biggest mistake that a Christian could ever made. It's when we fall for the trick of the enemy that, and we went to God crying ask God "Why" and it's already too late.

Remember the Bible never described the devil as an ugly thing with horn like they're showing you at the movies today. His name was Lucifer and he was described like a bright morning star. The reason why I take my time to share this with you is to let you know that the handsome fellow that saw you and think that he loves you can be your worst nightmare. After meeting him you might wish that you were never born, and never met him.

Don't let the flesh deceive you. Be strong, and say to yourself that "you're can resist the temptation with the help of Christ. "After getting myself into this mess I never thought that I could ever trust a man ever in my life because I thought that they're all the same, and then I learned to trust God in my decisions. My point is please do not let your eyes deceive you; it's not worth it to go through this pain let God perfect will to be done to your lives. Just because God let you do what your desires doesn't mean that is a good thing to you. It's not everything that is coming from God therefore be very careful. I will never take a decision without God ever again, and I believed that God will bless me with a man of God that's know the value of a woman and to treat me with respect as the princess that I am.

The reason why I mention me as a princess is because my father is the King of Kings. Women, or girls know your value in other for men not to treat you like trash. You worth more than that, but you need to know that in order for men not to treat you badly. And if a man told you that he loves you send him to read 1 Corinthians 13:4-7 to know the true meaning of love. Have a seat with him and open your Bible with him in this passage 1 Corinthians 13 even you will learn something about love.

I feel so happy and at the same time I also feel devastated, reason, I am so happy because I had to visit Orlando Florida once again. I really loved it in Orlando. When I came to the United States Orlando was the first state that lived for three years. I have a lot of friends there and my former pastor and his wife also still live there, and I was thinking of going for visit to share my testimony with those who didn't know about my accident. I'm willing to share my testimony everywhere in the world, so I asked my dad for my former pastor's phone number, and he gave it to me.

As I contacted my former pastor on what's up I told him that I would love to come visit Orlando, and he mentioned to me that one of the church member is getting married; it would be nice if I could come to visit, so I told him cool I called my dad to tell him that I want to go to her wedding. My dad told me "it is not up to him; it is up to me and I told him ok because I felt like I have his approval. Having a trust fund was a good thing for me because they took good care of my money. If that money was in my care, it would've been over already, but when my dad signs up to put the money in trust fun for me, I didn't understand at first, but now I do. I criticize them first and now I tried to understand all the facts of having a trust fun. I called my trust fund people to make a reservation, and they made it for me. I was so happy because after nine years, I'm finally going to visit Orlando. I was so happy for getting everything just because I had gone back in Orlando.

I even tell my friends to keep me in their prayers for the vacation to go well. What make me sad this afternoon is that I've been telling my Jersey friends if God wants me to move back to Orlando may His will be done. I felt like all pains start when I moved to Jersey; that was so selfish of me because the pains that I have in Jersey was the reason why I know who Christ Jesus really is. Because of these pains Christ finally got the way that He wanted me to be meaning the servant that He wants me to be.

My life is not my own anymore I can't just do whatever I want with it. Truly I was thinking of everything that I'm going through, and feel so tired of them. If it was my will I would've just move out of New Jersey, and then again, I feel like if do so it is like I'm running away from the trials. It is not me to run away from difficulties. Then again I said to myself "you're only think like that because of emotions; do not let your emotions make you think like that. In my emotions or whatever it was I even said that 'when I was in Orlando, I never went through those suffering like I do in New Jersey.

I want to have peace in my mind; peace in my spirit and peace in myself." I want to be free from all the disasters I go through because I am the one who brought them to myself. There is no one to blame but myself seriously as human I am very tired of them, but as a servant of God Philippians 4:12-13 says that I know what it is to be in need, and I know what it is to be plenty. I have learned the secret of being content in every situation, whether living in plenty or in want. I love the 13 verse that says I can do all this through Him who gives me strength.

In my experience with Christ, I would say that "I am an overcomer through Christ who gives me a second chance of life to live again. Even when I didn't deserve it. Thank God who is a faithful, and a compassionate God. God is the only person who truly love me I know that for sure after what I've been through. He shows it to me in every way.

I have an appointment for my driving test; I spoke to the transportation manager for two weeks ago about it, and he told me "Ok no problem." I know for sure that everything is going to just fine. This afternoon March 8 I asked the transportation if I set up for my appointment, and he told me no; I am so disappointed about that because I don't know how am I getting to my appointment, so I cried ask God please help.

As I'm writing this something come to me in my heart "Why are you so worried about that? Don't you know that God is your provider? And I find my strength again, and I said that since I have a credit card, I will call a cab to bring me there. I hope I pass that test because it is very difficult for me, but God always have a plan I believe that God is going to help me with it by faith I already pass that test.

Unfortunately, I didn't go to the appointment because the group home told me that they are not responsible for that kind of appointment because it wasn't a doctor's appointment. So, I decided to apply for a transportation for disabled, so I could go to my next appointment. I knew that I had a doctor's appointment also the beginning of the month, but they didn't bring me. This morning I received a letter from the doctor because I missed the appointment, so I will bring them the letter today in order for them to reschedule my doctor's appointment for me.

One more excitement tomorrow is my break to go to Orlando Florida after ten years. I didn't call my going to Orlando a vacation, but a mission to share my testimony with the people over there. I had a lot of friends over there, but they do not know about my accident. I am so happy to go share my testimony with the people of Orlando Florida because New Jersey knows about my accident, and my testimony is for all the World to know what God did for me; God can do it for them as well if they believe.

In Hebrews 13:8 says that Jesus Christ is the same yesterday and today and forever. It's true people have faith in God "you will see what I'm telling you and what the Bible says about God is real. In order when those people see my accident pictures and me standing to testify what God has done for me is real. If there were some people that come to church just to come play game in order for them to stop what they're doing, and to start living the life that Christ wants them to live. What God wants from us as a Christians. In 1 Thessalonians 4:2-7 explain it all.

A Christian's life is not just to come to the sanctuary, but God wants us to be sanctify at all time. Live a purify life for Christ. Have the same mindset as Christ Jesus. Apostle Paul said that in Philippians 2: 5. Always make the Words of God your best friend, and you will see what's going to accomplish in your life. Read Joshua 1:8 to see. God bless you all.

Today the 22ⁿᵈ of March before my travel to Orlando Florida the next day; I had a group of sisters come to pray with me. I really enjoy the prayers and the company of them; my sisters in Christ God bless them. Thank God I had a great time in Orlando; Jesus was with me all the way since the first day that I left and the day that I got back. He was my pilot when I left for Orlando Florida, and He was my pilot in my way back.

I gave my testimony everywhere I went: in the Supermarkets, the street. the beauty salon, and every church that I visited. I don't call myself visitor when I go to a church because in the house of the Lord, I am not a visitor. It's a home to me; I was so happy to go back there after nine (9) years, and the people over there was so happy when I testified to tell them that just like Hebrews 13:8 says Jesus Christ is the same yesterday and today and forever. They saw it when I stand to talk for the Lord, and when they saw my accident pictures.

I visited all the places that I knew when I lived there; I shared my testimony with them. They were surprise to see me remembering everything after my brain injury. That's how awesome God is. He gave me a better memory after a terrible brain injury. There is nothing impossible for God to do. Raisin people from the death I repeat nothing. I want to go back to school so bad that's why I applied for transportation to attend Campus.

I also want to renew my license in order for me to go back to all my regular activities such as 'go back to school, and to go back to my church activities, go back to work. 'I want to change my major to Social worker and Psychology because I love helping people. I also love to talk to people helping them with their issues. I went back to school, and graduated as a social science in June 2019, and admitted to Kean University to pursue my goal as a psychologist.

I want to be a marriage counselor; some people told me that I have to be married to be a marriage counselor, but I hope it's going to be a problem really. The thing is I was not ready to be a wife because I didn't have any role model as a married couple, but now since I am in God school He instruct me how to be a submissive wife. I learned that from the Bible in the book of Ephesians 5 Apostle Paul explains how a wife should be with her husband and how a husband should treat his wife.

I think I'm ready now to be a wife. To be the wife of the man God created for me. That man will show me the love that I believe in, which is "the true love;" the reason why I was so scared is because men now and then all they do is tricking women because they said that women are the weakest sex "all they have to do is just to convince a woman by telling her the 'L' word, and the she will fall for it that's why I was so hard on any man that used this word to me because I always think that he's lying. Imagine 10 men come to you and use that word to you every second that petrified me so much because really it's a lie. They don't even know you; they just meet you and they're already in love with you.

That's why I was so scared, but I know that God will send me a man he doesn't even have to say the word I would see it in eyes, and I will understand. I will tell you more when I meet him because he is out there for me, and I believe it will happen just the way I expect it to be. You know sometimes you can tell if someone is lying to you just by looking at him; that's me I can't be fool twice. Fool me once; it's ok but fool me twice it's a shame on you.

I've learned something very important in God school; I learned how to salute somebody's time. When a wind blows in someone's life just be happy for them because it's their time. For the past month I've been asking God for wisdom because I felt lack of it. James 1: 5 says If any of you lacks wisdom, you should ask God, who gives generously to all without finding fault, and it will be giving to you.

I believe that received the wisdom that I asked God for. Who knows when my wind blow what's going to happen. That song keep on coming to my heart every second "Christ have a surprise for you" and I believe in this words; I'm waiting for my wind to blow, and thank God for everybody that have the wind blow for them already. I salute their winds because when my wind blow I don't know what will it be, but I believe something greater will happen in my times that's why I asked God for a lot of patients to wait and to be happy for somebody that already have their wind blow for them.

People that are reading this will always have a positive attitude. Be positive something greater will happen in your life in the future no matter what happen to you in the past. Do not lose hope our God is greater than everything that we do not understand now surely, we will understand, when stuff happen in your lives "do not ask God why?" Things happen for a reason; we may not understand it now, but later in the future we will understand. Remember what Romans 8:28 says about that God bless you all that are reading all the advices that in my book, and think about it God has a great plan for all our lives; be patient that's all it takes.

Your surprise will come from above; do not trouble yourself over nothing because Jesus says in John 16:33 He have overcome the world for us already, and do not give the devil access to your lives a little thing can bring him to your lives; things that you think it's just a small things, but a small thing is what it takes for him to find his way to your life's. "James 4:7 says Submit yourselves, then, to God. Resist the devil, and he will flee from you. Be careful on the small things that come to your lives don't think of them as the smallest things ever because James also says it takes a small spark to set a forest on fire just like the tongue is a small part of the body, but it makes great boast.

Sometimes you can kill somebody with your tongue, and not even realize it. James 3:5-6 explain it all read the book of James, and you will find out how dangerous our tongue is. You cannot say just anything with your mouth because the same mouth that "Bless can also curse." Be careful with what's coming out of your mouths. This afternoon Roman 12 start with the 11 verses until the 21st come to my heart where Paul talks about love how to love everybody even those who persecute you.

Jesus loves those who was crucified Him; He even ask God the father to forgive them what about us we need to forgive one another as Christ has forgiven us and love one another. God is love if you call yourself a servant of God act like one. Let God have His way in you. Let's Him do what He please with you may, and His Will be done to your lives. The scripture also talks about to bless those who persecute you; bless and do not curse. It's good to love "love as much as you can" it's not easy to love those who hate you, but with God strength you will love like Christ love, and forgive you.

If you really want the strength to do so just ask God for it, and He will give it to you. I'm telling you that because I've been through it; things were not always easy for me instead of holding grudges I asked God to strengthen me, and He gave me the strength that I needed. Thank you, Lord. I asked God to put joy in my heart always because in Proverbs 17:22 says A cheerful heart is good medicine, but a crushed spirit dries up the bones, and He did all I did was asked Him for joy not only that; I asked Him to install joy in my heart that's the reason why I always have a smile on my face. I never had to fake my smile; it's always true, and I'm always happy even in my darkest moment. I used to cry a lot when those moment present themselves, and now not anymore because God put a joy in my heart that I don't even know how to explain. If He did it for me He can do it for you as well believe me.

I'm not sharing anything to you that I didn't go through. Please don't be jealous, or envy of anything that somebody own. It is his /or hers just be happy for them instead of being jealous. it's not your time yet when your time come you will know because God will bless openly for even your enemies to see your deliverance, and be put to shame because of the humiliation that they used give you. God will lift you up right through their faces, and they will regret the way they've been treated you.

I applied for an online school at Argosy University for BA in Psychology (Bachelor of Art in Psychology) and after the human resources I want to be a marriage advisor. One of the people that I shared that with told me that they are not going to accept me in this program because I'm not married. I told her I don't think it's fair if I am good at what I'm doing what does it has to do with being married?

I know that I'm not married, but it has nothing to do with me being a marriage counselor if I am good at it. You never heard of a mature adult that is not married; that's me and I attended the best University ever its name is "GU" stand for God University and my professor is Jesus Himself. I know that many of you would not understand, but it's true in my experience with God I was in His class that taught me a lot about life. I don't expect for any of you to understand, but it's true. In God University I learned how to be a humble person, a submissive wife, a respectful person in general etc... Like I said before I wasn't ready to be a wife because I wasn't raise by married people, but even though I wasn't raised by one I end up knowing it all in GU. Now I'm ready for it because I have the best teacher ever, and I've learned so much under His teaching.

I don't know if you guys ever heard of a mature single person I don't like to brag, but I consider myself as one of them because I've grown so much in God University, and I am so happy to attend His University. I consider myself a lucky one to attend His University; be smart people register in God University believe me you would not regret the choice you made at GU. You will see the different between all Universities that you're attended. By experience I know exactly what I'm referring you to trust me.

I was a horrible human being before attended GU, but now I'm a new person because even though I was a Christian 2 Corinthians 5:17 was never done in my life. After attending GU I've been transformed and finally 2 Corinthians 5:17 is in my life. Thank God; I've talked to a College advisor yesterday the 16 of April regarding me wanting to be a Psychologist as a marriage counselor because of what my friend told me. She told me that "it is not true of what my friend told if I'm not married they're not going to accept me in College to be a marriage advisor.

I was so happy when the advisor told me that to do not bother of what people are saying about what I want to do with my life as long I love what I do. The thing is people are worried about money, but I care about helping people who are need for help. It's not about money as long that I'm helping people it's enough for me. I was taking the Register Nurse; it was not because I like it, but because that's what my family want me to do. Now I want to stop living of what people want from me, but of what I really love to do as long as I am good of it.

Does he know what he's saying? Because I believe in true love, and I also believe that God has a prince for me somewhere therefore I'm not in a hurry to put myself into something that would get me hurt again. In the previous chapter I explain to you guys how I got myself into a big mess meaning "I got a major brokenhearted by my ex-best friend. Until now I am so scared to let anybody in my life because I'm still scared of what happened to me before.

I remember using a proverb about a cat burnt from a hot water and see a cold water and he flee far from it because he thinks that he's going to burn from it as well 'that's what happened to me I am very careful in that case because I don't want the same thing to happen to me. I'm so scared in that matter therefore I put my life completely in God hands for His Will to be done in my life. Life like I experienced before was not so good, or so easy to me in that case.

I now understand what a true love is. A true love is the love that God shows me when that happened to me until now through my accident. God still have mercy on me even though I didn't deserve that love. I didn't even invited Him before I made that decision, but He saw what I was going through and His eyes was on me.

When I say that I love God believe me I really do. A mighty God like that deserves all the love from the bottom of my heart. That's the reason why I give myself to Him to do what He please with me. The point of all this is to love someone is by showing it in action. God show His love for me when I didn't deserved it, so I encourage everybody to love without interest. Love is not to defend your interest from somebody by that I mean "just because someone have a pretty face, and want to sleep with that person, so he uses the word; it's not really true.

Sometimes when the girl say it back to him "he ask just prove it to show me that you're really mean it." When he says to prove it that could only mean one thing; to make out with him once you start making out with he knows you can't resist the temptation therefore he will want something more. When I say something more you know what exactly I mean by that; you have to finish what you started by end up sleeping with him which sooner or later you will regret it.

In fact love is not a game just because you want something from that person, so you use the words love just to get what you want. You can find the meaning of love in 1 Corinthians 13. When you read that chapter in the New Testament from the Bible write by the Apostle Paul and understand it now you will be able to know what love it's all about, and be ready to express your love to someone. After knowing the true meaning of love you will stop using the word in vain, and when you propose to somebody because of the true meaning of it believe me you will have a successful marriage.

Knowing one another

The question is "How would you know one another?" For me is to take time to have a connection of soul with that future spouse of yours. By that I mean to date that person in order to know if that person have a good /or bad quality. What that person like or dislike? What attract you to that person? If you can spend your entire life with that person to respect your commitment to one another. Most of the marriage fail because you didn't take time to really know what you're getting yourself into when you take the engagement to spend your life with that person.

It's very important to know these things about your future significant one; the thing is you are two different person who were raised in two different environment. Most of the time we in a hurry to get married because our friends are getting married which is so wrong. You don't know how and what your friends do to get married to that person; his or her time might come before you; just be happy for them. Don't think because they're getting married; you have to rush into marriage just because you met someone you feel like you have to get married without knowing that person first.

Be patient to wait for your time, and when your time come believe me you're not going to regret because what God has for you is much greater than what you're rushing yourself into. You don't even know what is into marriage I spoke to some married people about marriages; they said to me marriage is not easy the way it seems to be. Sometime you attend your friend wedding, but you don't know what they're going through in their marriages after the commitment they made before God and before every body.

I know some people after years of marriage because they didn't really know each other well, and got married just because they're aging which is not a reason to put yourself into marriage. They end up arguing after they have the kids in their marriages. When they have kids they're still arguing even right in front of their kids which is not a good idea. They even physical fight in front of the kids, and they said that "they will love one another until death 'do us part'.

I asked a married woman that question "didn't you stand before God and the pastor saying 'yes to that statement, and she said to me it was the pastor who said the word she just agreed with the pastor. That's sad; very sad. She was in a hurry to get married because she was in her late thirties so she just choose to marry the first man that come. Therefore I could say that she was so impatient to wait for God's Will, and she prayed that dearly.

To understand one another

To understand one another is to try not to change each other and learn to deal with each other's differences. Never go to bed mad at each other; even when something's not right always talk it out and make up even if it takes all night. If you start out the next day still mad at each other it may grow bigger, so kiss and make up. It's good to talk have a real conversation like never before. Laugh at each other's jokes. Wife "it doesn't have to be a special day; make your husband breakfast in bed. You can still wear your night gown to bring him breakfast in bed. Be spontaneous you can also change to wear something sexy for your husband; nothing is wrong with that.

Communication

Always communicate with one another; have a deep conversation with your spouse. It's healthy to do so. Looking at each other's eyes to express your love toward one another every second you get a chance. Even try to remember your first date before you got married; what made you smile that day. Explain to each other how he/she made you feel so special that day, and since then you know from the bottom of your heart that you were meant to be together forever.

Tell her /him the happiest that you have been is when you first talk with each other, and start dating. Express the feelings you had how you always wish to meet your prince/princess, and here he/she comes out of nowhere. Tell one another that "you were always scared to lose his /

her company someday." How do you feel his/her love for you is when you're holding hand, and he put his arm around you. You feel so safe with him especially when he's looking right to your eyes. You can feel the love from his eyes.

Loyal And Trust

Loyal and Trust. Listen to one another stories. Sometimes your past stories are not beautiful, but talk to one another about that in order for him /her not to hear it from someone else. The reason why it is so important to talk about your ugly past with your mate before getting married is because you're not the same person anymore. And she /he needs to know that you're not like that anymore in order to trust each other. Do not lie to each other ever no matter how hard the truth is to you just tell your spouse the truth.

Believe me it will help your relationship toward one another. Besides the Bible tell us that Jesus is the truth, and the devil is a liar since the beginning. If you are for the truth Jesus is your father, but if you are lying you have for father the devil. Check John 8:44 to see what the Bible says about lying. Don't give one another any reason to do mistrust each other. Keep your love life alive by conversate with each other constantly. And woman always makes your husband feel the love that you have for him from the first day from the first day you got married; show him that the love never died. You know what your husband like just do whatever it takes to make your love renew every day just like the mercy of God that renew every morning.

If you don't do that and he's going to find another woman to light his fire on because you don't do your job, and you're not going to like that. Even when you're cooking in the kitchen, and you know what time he's coming home wear something sexy in the kitchen to have his attention after a day at work. Kiss him ask him how was his day? Do the same when you wake up in the morning as well. Great him ask him how was his night? because you might sleep in the same bed, but you don't know the dreams that he/she had over the night.

Respect

Respect is very important in a marriage. If you ask me what is more important in a marriage Love or respect? I will answer respect because if you don't respect one another it is impossible to find love in this relationship when you respect your partner, you understand she/he is a unique human being. So when you learn to respect each other both of you can work your relationship towards one another. He might like loud music and you like quiet music the point I gave you about understanding one another, and knowing one another if you use those points. You will know how to deal with each other when you use those points, and how to be a loving supportive mates for each other.

Honesty

You need to be honest in everything like communication. Communication takes a lot of work; how often have you walked away from a conversation with your partner feeling angry, disappointed or misunderstood? To avoid the fight in your marriage sometimes it's better to walk away because you might come to a point where you said something that you might regret later one. It is not worth it, so when your partner is angry at something that you do it's better not to answer. Wait until your partner calm down and communicate with him in a calmly voice. Even you're not guilty just tell him/her how sorry you are and this will never happen again.

That doesn't make you weak it makes a better person. How often have you said things you regretted? Things that hurt your partner unnecessary. How often have you wished for more open and honest communication with the person you love the most? The person that you make a commitment with for better or for worst you will be with. Don't say like the woman told me "it wasn't her words" it was the pastor's word, so she just agreed with the pastor.

Know one thing you don't make the commitment only before the pastor and the congregation, but first before God. That is why you must know your partner before making that commitment. By know your partner I don't mean to intimate with him just like people in this world say "to know somebody is to bed with that person before marriage. It's like I explain in the paragraph about "knowing one another by dating the person first" to know where you're putting yourself. Can that person be your spouse?

I hear some people say that the truth is hurt, but truth never hurt do not hesitate to tell your partner the truth about something that you don't like. Be honest about whatever you did wrong because it's better for you to tell her/him before he/she found out from somebody else. Transform the way we talk to each other by being "timely, flexible, patient, intuitive, accepting, honest." Being honest is the most important thing you can bring to your communication with your partner. Speak your truth, as much as you are able to with clarity, love and gentleness.

When you communicate your truth from a place of love, you're always reinforcing the strength of your connection with your partner. No matter the response you get from your partner; you have to be honest always. Communication can make or break a relationship. The more open and connected the dialogue, the healthier a relationship tends to be. That was the reason why my ex-best friend used to say that I'm mean. The thing is I am not mean but honest I don't like to be lying to therefore I will be upfront to tell you the truth. I would never like for somebody else to let my life secret to you that is why I always tell the story of my life to my friend.

You see when I talk about my past relationship I always say "my ex-best friend." The reason is very clear; he never knew that we were in a relationship therefore I was the only one in it, so I could not say that he was my boyfriend. No matter how close we were that make me think that I got played. Imagine someone you opened yourself to, and trust say that thing about you make everybody think that you're crazy.

In my experience it's really hurt, but I couldn't say anything because my parents didn't know what was going on between him and me. They only saw me with him always, but know nothing. It was not because I didn't want them to know I couldn't explain to them what was going on because the way he acted I didn't know or understand where I was. Let me not ever talk about that thing ever again. It was the past, so I don't even want to think about it.

Compromise

When it comes to compromise with your spouse before you take a decision ask your wife/husband what is he/she thinks about whatever it is? Consult your spouse always about your decisions before making them. What you think is good idea that's not what your mate thinks good. Learn how to compromise in your marriage. When you do that the commitment you make before God and before the pastor you will keep these promises "till death do us parts will be a success in your marriage". Speak up if you feel that something is happening that you don't agree with.

By speak up I don't mean for you to argue about it, but softly say how you feel about the situation. Offer your opinions, and tell her /him how you would like a certain things. Don't present yourself as a chief, or demanding because the Bible says in Proverbs 15:1 A gentle answer turns away wrath, but a harsh word stirs up anger. This statement is for women because sometimes we as women intended to wear the pants in the marriages which is not a good idea. Let the men keep their pants on; the men have priority over you because God give it to them. Ask yourself this question "Why did God chose the rib bond of a man to made the woman?" My answer is because God did it in other for us to know that we are equal and men have the right over everything in the house just like women do (Ephesians 5:15 -21,22-33).

Foundation

Before enter to the next key which is foundation; I have something very important to say about men and women who are abusing their spouse. Some men take pleasure in abusing their wives; beating on them, and physically, and mouthful. The Bible didn't say that God took a member of your foot to make the woman so you can step on her whenever you want to of, but instead It says that God took the bond ribs to make the woman. That's mean you are equal; do not treat your woman as a doormat, so you can step on her every time you want to. That's for the men, and women do not abuse your man with your mouth because I know that you can have a big mouth. Make peace among one another and respect one another because the Bible says in Ephesians 5:28-30 clearly you are members of Christ's body.

To build a Spiritual foundation in a marriage is very important. If you want to grow strong, one of the most important questions you and your spouse should answer is, How are we going to grow spiritually as a family? God created marriage, it is not merely two people in a relationship, but three -a husband, a wife, and God. Falling to address this question can almost guarantee that your marriage will not achieve the intimacy and oneness that God designed.**(Family Life; Building a Spiritual Foundation for your Marriage).**

The three keys for how to build a Spiritual Foundation for your Marriage are:

*1. **Is your family part of God's family**
*2. **Are both of you giving Christ control**
*3. **Are both of you allowing the Holy Spirit to guide and empower your lives?**

More of the keys to have success in your marriage.

1. **Don't put your marriage on a pedestal.** Every marriage struggles with shortcomings. In the early years of our marriage, I thought that we were supposed to be an almost perfect model for others. But I quickly learned that people don't need to see a flawless marriage. They need to see a couple asking for God's help as they deal with their shortcomings and weaknesses. When God brings two sinful people together, it's *war*. But God is the God of the supernatural, and He will give you the wisdom and strength to make the relationship work. Your children don't have to see you as perfect dad or mom all they need to see is a perfect example of you as parents. They need to see you dealing with your imperfections so they will know how to deal with their own imperfections.

2. **Do for your spouse what you want him or her to do for you.** Consider the consequences of your words and actions. Just like I mentioned "Ask yourself how you would want to be spoken to, or treated, or cared for. And then do those things. The Bible paraphrase, *The Message*, says in Luke 6:37-38, "Don't pick on people, jump on their failures, criticize their faults—unless, of course, you want the same treatment. Don't condemn those who are down; that hardness can boomerang. Be easy on people; you'll find life a lot easier. Give away your life; you'll find life given back, but not merely given back—given back with bonus and blessing. Giving, not getting, is the way. Generosity begets generosity."

3. **Recognize your differences and be willing to defer to one another.** Your spouse is not just like you. Learn to live with your differences. When I was growing up; I wasn't raise by my mom and dad therefore I don't know how having a family supposed to be, but as I was growing up by watching movies about how true love should be I always want it. Some people said to me "it's just entertainment" as a Christian I always believed that the type of true love God has it for me. Therefore, I never discourage because I believe that one day Mr. right will come For me at the right time. I never feel pressured to just to choose a man by myself because I am a strong believer who

relied on God for a perfect mate. I know that he will come because God made a promise upon my life and I believe in it. It will come to pass at the right time.

To be like that you need to be very patient, and I pray for patience from God every day. They are a lot to learn as a young girl who want to have a family someday; I had so much to learn for somebody who didn't raise with my mom and dad. That's the reason I chose to be a marriage counselor. I went to (GU) God's University that's why I know much about marriage. You see, there's a lot of give and take in a healthy marriage. There is a lot to learn before enter into marriage. Don't rush into marriage just because all your friends are doing it. Marriage it's not easy therefore take your time and analyzed all the facts before enter into marriage. Things like the differences you have and your spouse. So instead of dwelling on how different you are from your spouse, think about the things you have in common. And be willing to give up your preferences for one another.

4. **Remember that deep friendship is a key to true intimacy.** These days, you see a lot of sex in the media, as though it's the glue to a lasting marriage. But sex is not the key to an enduring bond between a husband and wife. You have to become friends first. And what do friends do? They spend time together doing things they both enjoy. When you see Cynthia or me, you usually see the other. And at the end of the day, we try to look at each other and remember, *you are my friend.*

5. **Love unconditionally, the way God loves you.** The only way that you can unreservedly love your spouse is by putting Jesus Christ at the center of your relationship. He can help you care for your spouse without expecting anything in return (1 Corinthians 13:4-7). I like to compare God's *agape* love in marriage to flying an airplane. The reason the plane overcomes gravity is because it's built according to the laws of aerodynamics (the way air moves around things). What happens if the plane loses power? The natural law of gravity will take over and the plane will begin to fall.

Likewise, in marriage, the moment you stop relying on God to help your marriage is the moment the natural law of selfishness takes over. The result? Division ... and too often, divorce.

6. **Don't think that you are above sin**. You are a sinner, just like every human being. But be encouraged. Jesus was tempted just like you and me. He wants to help us escape temptation (1 Corinthians 10:13). You will and your spouse have to face a lot of challenges— The challenges are a parts of life what you need to keep in mind; the challenges are just like a trail. You need to ask God for strength to face them. I know that all of you who are reading my essay are not Christians, but try to read the Bible references that I give you to see if I'm lying. We often have to humble ourselves and ask each other for forgiveness; humbling yourself to ask for forgiveness is the best way to have a healthy marriage even if you are right, and your spouse is wrong.

   Don't focus on the struggles, the weaknesses, or even the strengths in your marriage if you want to have a healthy marriage. Instead try to park on the sufficiency of God's grace even the unbelievers God is great, and if you believe that He can help you "He will".

7. **Love each other without demands.** When couples bring rules into a marriage—"This is your responsibility, not mine," or "I've done my part, now you do yours"—that usually reflects a loss of intimacy. Dr. Howard Hendricks, who was a beloved professor at Dallas Theological Seminary, said the more intimate the relationship, the fewer the rules that are necessary to regulate the relationship. True love is not demanding. It does not keep score or consider who does more work. In the Gant household, when either of us sees something that needs to be done, we do it.

8. **Do not get into debt.** You and your spouse can have chosen to have a simple lifestyle, and that philosophy has transferred to your children. They haven't seen you constantly battling over things that are here today and gone tomorrow. Part of your commitment has been to live without debt. When you have no credit card debt. No car debt. One car is 6 years old; another is 10 years old, and they

get you where you need to go. You just made choices to live with less and are glad we did. It makes for a more peaceful life.

The secret to our success

After almost years of marriage if you follow these advice carefully you can have success in your marriage. You would bring true unity that Jesus Christ want you to have into any relationship. And believe that, with Christ's help, your marriage will be even better tomorrow … and then the day after that.

I love the 29 verse that says: After all, no one ever hated their own body, but they feed and care for their body, just as Christ does the church. Think about it I know some have big mouth; my advice to you single people I know that sometimes you feel lonely, you end up making a decision without God which is a bad Idea because you suffer dearly in the future. In everything put God first even in the things you think it's just a little thing; you will how big it is when you get yourself in big trouble.

God knows what are good for us; He talk to us through the preachers, and even talk to us clearly in our dreams instead of asking God what does He trying to show us we just act like it nothing "oh it just a dream and then we forget about it. You know that God spoke to us in many ways if you don't understand what God is trying to show us don't trust yourselves. Go to God in prayers to ask Him what does He trying to show you. I don't why am I end up writing about that especially as a single woman since when the ideas come to me it is not what I please to put in I write what God put in my heart in it. You need to know that I don't just write to write I write what God put in my heart sometimes He wakes me up in the middle of the night just to write. I can't say nothing because it is His will that I'm doing.

I encourage you guys to do what please God because God knows past, present, and future. Do not ever plan your future without consulting God because God knows the future before it presents itself. He is Omnipotent, Omnipresent, and Omniscient. In James 4:13-15

It says you do not know what will happen tomorrow, what tomorrow will bring instead say if it is in God's Will because of the time we plan everything ahead. Who knows if we're going to see the night or the second after the hour that you make the plans, or tomorrow.

Only Almighty God knows, and if you goes by His Will believe me He plans your lives in the palm of His hand, and He command His Angels to protects you in every ways. Read Psalms 91:7-12 to see what it says; the words of God is always truth. The Bible says in Numbers 23:19 God is not human, that He should lie, not a human being, that He should change His mind. Does He speak and then not act? Does He promise and not fulfill? Think about all the scriptures what they says about God, and ask yourself that question "when did God ever say something without fulfill it? then answer the question in yourselves.

Like I mentioned earlier Do not rush in doing something without God say "yes, or no you can't? Sometimes we make a decision, and we know that God is not in it, yet we still do it because you trust in yourself, and in your feelings think that is what God wants for you; I can tell you one thing "you are lying to yourself, and you will dearly in the future. Trust God and everything will be just the way they supposed to be. That's just a suggestion therefore you might take it or not; it's really up to you. In other words that I can simplify my point to our you people.

Please do not rush into marriage just for "sex" because there is more in marriage then sex. You're about to put yourself in serious trouble if "sex" is the reason that you want to get married. Sex is a part of it, but it is not supposed to be the main reason. Think about it like that "I want to get married because God created me to spent my life with someone that He created for me. Because God says that in Genesis 2:18 (The Lord God said, "It is not good for man to be alone. I will make a helper suitable for him.") Let God give you the person that He created for you.

We as human being most of the time we make poor decisions because our flesh wants what it wants, and feel like we have to pleasure our flesh. Let the Spirit of God take over the flesh Galatians 5:16-21 explain what will happen when you're going the flesh desires, so let the Spirit of God lead you to the right path because our flesh is a big deceiver. If you're listening to it; you'll be doomed, and you don't want that. You don't know when Jesus is coming back, so be careful. For some reason I don't feel like developing the next Key which is "Foundation, but to thank God for my life and the trials that He trust me to go through."

I remembered that God before starting this chapter; God made a complete silence, but it wasn't the end of the book. Even I didn't know if there was another chapter to come, and since God was the one who gave me the directions to write whatever that I wrote in it. Therefore when it was time to write this chapter God Himself told me to start writing it, and what to write about. I honestly didn't know much about marriage, and yet I end up writing about marriage. What happened was I went to the bathroom to take a shower, and the voice talk to my heart that it was time to write "chapter four in my book, and I didn't know what was I going to write about?" And the voice told me that to write about "The keys to a successful marriage."

The voice also gave me the keys to write about, and I did what the voice told me to write. To tell you the truth I went to a point where my flesh was so strong; I said to myself that I'm done crying because of that matter, and I do not want to go back doing what God against meaning (masturbation). Therefore, I had signed myself to three dating website which I was against before, and I promise myself never to do. When I came to my senses and said to myself "what is God cannot do for you" God knows and aware of your needs.

He is preparing the right man for you, so why do you feel so desperate to get a man on your own? You remembered what happened to you before when you let your flesh deceived you by tricking you on chosen someone by yourself. And what happened to you? I deleted all the websites at the moment and realized that if God rose me from death there is nothing that He won't do for me. I waited for God to send me the man that He created for me because God never rush, and His plans are always perfectly accomplished in its time. I rebuke the devil plans for making think like that in Jesus's name. The plan of God for my life I claim over my life Hallelujah! Amen!!!

So, I prayed for God to strengthen me to calm my flesh down before He send me my significant one that He's preparing for me. This morning I remembered when the Holy Spirit guided me to John 16; I remembered reading the 16 verses that talk about "The Disciples' Grief will turn to Joy" I said to myself why did I do that desperate thing when God has a promise over my life? My prayers before God was "God please give me a lot of strength in my weaknesses. I really need you in this matter and I promise never dare to do anything like that ever again in Jesus's mighty name. Amen and Amen!!!!!!

I'm so grateful for the life that God gives me and the opportunity to start a brain new life all over. In that life He renew my memories even the things that passed in my life after six years I still remember them even stuff from when I was growing up. At a point I even remember everything that happened to me in the pass life of mine; I remembered it all. The Bible clearly says to do not even think about the former things in Isaiah 43:18-19 "Forget the former things; do not dwell on the past. In the 19 verse God says to the prophet Isaiah See, I'm doing a new thing! Now it springs meaning God has a perfect plan for our lives.

The funny thing is after I wrote about "The Keys Of A successful marriage" Coincidently I usually open my TV on Lifetime on Sunday before I go to Church at 8:30 (DR. David Jeremiah) was preaching about marriage, so the sermon was very interested I order the book about "What the Bible Says about; Love, Marriage & Sex" the book is very interesting I've learned so much about the subject. "I believe it's nothing yet because the best is yet to come; I start reading a book on "What the Bible says about; (Love, Marriage, and Sex writing by Dr David Jeremiah" I discovered a lot of information's in it.)

Today May 23rd 2016 was a great day for me because I finally get clear from my driving test thank God. I'm waiting for my trust fund to give me an answer of when can I go shopping for my car to return back to my church activities Hallelujah! Amen thank you Lord. I'm so excited!!!!! God is so good in my life; I can't complain about nothing, and thank God I'm not a complainer. Praise God!!!!!!! It is now I finally understand what the driving instructor mean when he didn't clear me from the driving test the first time.

It wasn't the right time because God fix the perfect time for me to get out of the driving test, but I didn't understand it the first time. Everyone cared about my safety on the road, but what I saw if you read the second chapter; you can see how angry that I was and described the man as a money hunger. I let my flesh and my emotions to make me act that way; now after passing the test I realized it and feel so sorry for letting my emotions go that far. God time is the best time! I went car shopping yesterday the 28th of May 2016, and get me a Pre-owned Chevy almost brand new.

I loved it so much; before I went for a Honda at the dealership, and I test drove a CRV Honda SUV'S, but I don't think that was the car that God want me to have because as I was test drove it to go out with it; I almost hit something right then I know it wasn't the car that God has for me. I didn't feel comfortable behind the wheel at all, and the dealer asked me: is Honda the car that you're looking for, and suggest another model to me I told him to bring it as he brought it I smiled because I took my driving test in a Chevy, so I asked him to test drive it my sister says "No she didn't think that I was ready to test drive yet based on what happened about the Honda that I was trying to test drive earlier. "I finally got the car that God has for me after walking a lot in the cold temperature 25 miles to 30 miles to attend fasting and prayers. That make me think one thing "the time was not yet come, and I believe sooner or later when the time comes no one could stop it.

The right time was the last week of January; I finally got my car, and I am free at last to participate in all my regular activities before my accident. God has done so much in the past four(4) years in my life even though I didn't get the car that I hope for, but I am so very happy with the car that I have now. I finally moved out of the group home, and get myself a car have my own apartment; it's all I wished for, and God grant them to me thank God. Praise His Holy name forever,

I agreed with her because she didn't understand what happened back there since I've been driving like forever; even I didn't understand it. I understand it when the man brought the Chevy to me, and he saw me smile again; I didn't test drive that car, so I let my sister to do it when we were done I told the man I want that car, and I got the car because something inside of me said "this is the car, and I got it." Hallelujah thank you Lord!!!!

After putting a deposit at the dealership to purchase the car; I had cognitive therapy with one of the therapist at the rehab, and I was so excited about getting the car I opened my big mouth to tell her about it. She thought that I paid too much money for the car like she was the one that is going to pay it for me, and she end up putting another person to my business which I didn't appreciate at all because I believe that Cog therapist with a client story should be confidential therefore the big bosses called me at a meeting. What they said to me that as long that I live in their property I can't own a car. Imagine how shocked I was?

So since I saw people who live in their apartment they drive to come to the rehab, so I asked them about getting one of their apartment; they told me that their apartment is not available right now. I asked them what if I get my own apartment? They told me that I can be an outpatient at the rehab; just because I had a brain injury they don't think I could live in an apartment by myself. I asked them why not? They told me it's not safe for me which I don't understand because they do not see me throwing rock at people "meaning that I'm not crazy.?

I told them that I will move with my brother since I've been paying them a money for no reason. I've got discharged from therapy since Mid last year 2015 because my family doesn't have a big house to put me therefore I have no choice, but to stay in their property. They told me that they can only bring me to a doctor's appointment only; they are not responsible to bring me anywhere else. I had an appointment with the driving school for my driving test therefore I'd missed that appointment., I applied for Access Link to bring me in the driving class when I got approve with Access Link in the second test I got cleared from the driving test.

Thank God because I passed the driving test in God's time. God's time is the best time. And I also believe that God fix a perfect time to get me out of their property, and God did. Know one thing as a TBI patient you are not really free no matter how old you are. They take control of your life and your decisions. What they say have to go the way they want it to go. I have one question for you that are reading my book "Do I sound crazy to you for somebody that had a traumatic brain injury?/TBI patient" I understand that I'm under their care, but that didn't give them to take my right from me.

Even to cook in their house I had to take a test. I let them know that "Cordon Bleu is the name that they used to call me before my accident" and if they do not know what the word mean I sent them to google the word, and they will find the meaning of it. The thing is they think that I'm a cuckoo because of my brain injury; they don't realized How great is My God Who rose me up from the death, and brought me so far from 2013 till 2016 what God has done in my life. If I was them, I would ask for That Jesus Christ Who still doing miracles today. Like Hebrews13:8 says, and explains how God's nature never change.

Because of my freedom they took from me I told them surely I will rent my own apartment, and they will never hear or see me again because I will get a job to rent my apartment. Even my old boss told me that if I came to apply for a job; she will give me a job there. I will call Access Link to bring me to work and bring me back to their house until I get enough money to rent an apartment. I'm 30 years of age so I can't turn into a baby that in diaper anymore; I'm not in a hurry but enough is enough. I'm not a complainer with patient I will on God for His purpose on my life.

I also believe that God doesn't bring me that far to leave me. God has the final say in my life because I belong to God, patiently I will wait on God. The lessons that I learned from those experience of my life are that; nothing is Eternal in this World that we're living in "not even a husband that made a commitment to you at the altar before God and before men if you don't invite God to the decisions that we are making in this life. Therefore always put God first in all of them because men can live you and forsake you; just like my ex-best friend did, but God promise us that He will never leave us nor forsake us.

A friend can say that they never knew you no matter how close you were with them, but remember they are human. Things happen with human even though they express themselves to you to tell you how much they love you every day; they could denied you in a second for another, but God will never do that. God is the only truth to everything if you want to know the true love in your lives just trust in God and you will experience the real love. And God can give you the mate that He himself created for you if you trust in Him. When you trust in God "you don't go make decisions by yourselves.

God knows everybody from head through toes (Psalms 139:2-4); He already know what you need before ask for it. God knows everything about us; when we need something come to Him with a sincere heart because sometimes we might want something, but that is not what you really need, or that's not what God want for us. God will grant what you really need not what you think that you want because there is a big differences between want and need. I will take my time to make sure you have the meaning of both words. The difference is "you may want something, but that's not what really need."

As google define it like this; Often times we confuse what we require and what we desire in relationships. We make a list of all the important traits we *want* in a partner, with very little concept of what we really *need* in our relationships. Our lists often include items about physical appearance, the level of income or career, and may end with a general statement like "they make me feel happy." I hate to break it to you, but you are the one that is responsible for ensuring that you are happy and your needs get met. It is up to you to understand what you need in a relationship versus what you want, and it is your responsibility to effectively communicate those things. Let's take a look at what constitutes a need.

Webster's defines a need as "something that a person must have: something that is needed in order to live, or succeed, or be happy." A need is something that is essential and very important to live a healthy and satisfied life. For years psychology has been trying to determine what these essential needs really are. Some of you might be familiar with Maslow's attempt to distinguish the order and importance of needs in his popular hierarchy as seen below.

"To want" something is just a desire that your flesh put in your mind, and when that desires come you will try anything to get. The question is "is it worth it?" Webster's defines a want as a desire or a wish for something. A want is something we might like to have rather than a requirement for healthy living. For example, I might want a man who drives an Audi R8. However, the car that my partner drives has very little impact on the emotional and psychological support they invest in the relationship. Most of you are probably agreeing with me thinking, "Obviously, you can't choose a man based on the car he drives!" You are right. But often times the differences between our needs and are wants are not as pronounced as this example. They walk a fine line and I dare say they even change from couple to couple.

I suspect that part of the reason that we confuse the two so easily is because our culture teaches us to be impulsive and listens to our urges. We were taught that "You Only Live Once" (YOLO), that you should "Just Do It" and to "enjoy the moment" … just to name a few. Advertising, marketing and music are constantly trying to reveal areas where we are deficient so that we believe that we *need* their products. Our relationships are not immune to these messages. We constantly feel like we need to be having more sex, be flawless looking for our partners, and are left with an aching feeling that we will never be enough.

There is a big difference between those two words please try to understand the differences, and trust God because your lives traced in the palm of His hands. That's how much God love us; He created everything before He created mankind. I Genesis 1:26 the Bible tells us that after He finished created everything in six day He said "Let us make mankind in our image, in our likeness, so that they may rule over the fish in the sea and the birds in the sky, over the livestock and all the wild animals, and over all the creatures that move along the ground."

God made provisions for us before He made mankind; therefore do not worried about things that you think that really want. Sometimes you're troubling yourself for something that you want, but what's important is the things that you need. God knows what we need let the perfect Will of God purpose in your lives. Like I mentioned there is a big difference between what we want and what we need: meaning / things that you think that you want. You see He created man first and He said that it is not good for the man to be alone then He created the woman to be a companion to the man. God made me famous overnight, and love it. Let me explain what I mean by that. Everyone knows my story where God took me from; I would call it the conclusion of "The Testimony Of My Life."

Printed in the United States
by Baker & Taylor Publisher Services